D0376556

A SHORT HISTORY OF

THE TROUBLES

**Four decades of violence have divided the people of
Northern Ireland – this book is an examination and
explanation of why and how this conflict happened.**

The Troubles have been in the news every day for the past
thirty-five years. The origins of the conflict are complex,
the evolution of the situation confusing, the effect of the
violence devastating. Here, Brian Feeney charts the descent
to violence and the progress towards peace. An insightful,
concise account of a troubling and often deeply confusing
situation.

'This history of the Troubles should be invaluable to those
who want to know about the Troubles quickly, to remind
those who went through it and, perhaps more importantly,
those who didn't of the whole gamut of human folly that
was the Troubles.' *Irish News*

BRIAN FEENEY is an historian, writer and political commentator. He is Head of History at St Mary's University College, Belfast, and formerly an SDLP councillor for north Belfast. As such, he experienced first-hand the effects of the Troubles on the lives of those living in Belfast. As a writer, his work has received awards and critical acclaim. He is co-author of *Lost Lives*, the definitive work on all those who died as a result of the Troubles, and he is the author of the best-selling *Sinn Fein, A Hundred Turbulent Years*, *16Lives: Seán MacDiarmada*, and (with Gerry Bradley) of *Gerry Bradley's Life in the IRA*. A columnist for the *Irish News*, Brian is a respected commentator on Northern Irish politics. He lives in Belfast.

Picture credits
The author and publisher thank the following for permission to reproduce images: **Front cover:** courtesy of Alain LeGarsmeur/Corbis; **Back cover montage:** images courtesy *Irish News*; **Picture section:** images courtesy of *Irish News*, p.3 (bottom), p.4 (top), p.6 (both), p.7 (bottom), p.8 (top); images courtesy of Pacemaker Press International, p.1 (bottom), p.2 (bottom), p.5 (both), p.7 (top), p.8 (bottom).
While every effort has been made to clear copyrights, if any error or omission has been made the copyright holder(s) should contact the publisher.

A SHORT HISTORY OF
The Troubles

Brian Feeney

THE O'BRIEN PRESS
DUBLIN

First published in smaller format 2004 by The O'Brien Press Ltd,
12 Terenure Road East, Rathgar, Dublin 6, D06 HD27, Ireland.
Tel: +353 1 4923333; Fax: +353 1 4922777
E-mail: books@obrien.ie
Website: www.obrien.ie
Reprinted 2005.
Updated edition published 2007.
Reprinted 2010.
This edition first published 2014.
Reprinted 2016, 2018.
The O'Brien Press is a member of Publishing Ireland.

ISBN: 978-1-84717-644-8

3 5 7 8 6 4
18 20 21 19

Editing, typesetting, layout and design: The O'Brien Press Ltd
Printed and bound by CPI Group (UK) Ltd, Croydon, CR0 4YY
The paper in this book is produced using pulp from managed forests.

Published in

DUBLIN
UNESCO
City of Literature

Contents

1. Reform and Reaction, 1963–1968

The deployment of British troops in 1969 to halt major civil strife on the streets of Derry and Belfast is commonly cited as the start of the Troubles. But Northern Ireland did not suddenly erupt into a clear blue sky in 1969. Whiffs of sulphur had been rising into the atmosphere for years. The first wisps appeared in 1963 as soon as the new leader of the permanent Unionist administration, Terence O'Neill, tried to initiate reform. The response to his efforts from both inside and outside his own party quickly demonstrated the truth of Alexis de Tocqueville's maxim that 'the most dangerous moment for an oppressive government is that at which it begins to reform'.

In March 1963 Terence O'Neill became only the fourth prime minister in the North of Ireland in forty-two years. O'Neill replaced the seventy-four-year-old Lord Brookeborough who had governed since 1943. Brookeborough, a dour old bigot from Fermanagh who had helped set up the loyalist militia, the B Specials, in 1920, had kept the North in deep freeze since the Second World War. Infamous for saying he would 'not have a Catholic about the place', he legitimised the endemic sectarianism of the Unionist regime.

Since the establishment of Northern Ireland by the Government of Ireland Act 1920, Unionist politicians had kept an iron grip on the six northeastern counties that the then British prime minister, Lloyd George, had carved out for them. The region was administered by a miniature government, complete with prime minister and Cabinet. There was a legislature made up of a fifty-two-member Commons and a smaller, powerless Senate. By judicious boundary changes, called gerrymandering, and by abolishing proportional representation, Unionists usually managed to win about forty of the seats in the Commons – an unassailable majority.

Unionists kept all levers of power in their own hands, completely excluding the minority Catholic community, also called nationalists, from all facets of the new State. Unionists regarded nationalists as disloyal and subversive. It should also be said that, in the early days of the regime, even if Unionists had offered any position to nationalist politicians it would have been refused because the nationalist community refused to recognise that the new arrangements had any legitimacy.

The political structures in the North were buttressed by a heavily armed police force, the Royal Ulster Constabulary (RUC), and a part-time, armed Protestant militia called the B Specials. Apart from the extensive range of firearms at their disposal, the most powerful weapon the security forces could deploy was the provisions of the Special Powers Act 1921, which gave police wide-ranging powers of search-and-arrest, detention without trial and, incredibly in a part of twentieth-century United Kingdom, flogging.

During the whole of the regime's existence prior to 1969 there was no Catholic Cabinet member. Most judges and magistrates and virtually all senior civil servants were Protestant. Indeed, many of the judges had previously been Unionist politicians before moving to the bench. To copper-fasten loyalty to the Unionist polity, anyone taking up a publicly paid job – police officer, teacher, civil servant, local government official – had to swear an oath of allegiance to the British Crown. Many nationalists refused to do this, as the Unionist legislators hoped they would.

Local government too was a Unionist preserve, with over 1,000 councillors elected in Northern Ireland. Although as many as one-quarter of the councillors were nationalists, the council areas were gerrymandered by boundary changes to ensure that nationalists never managed to gain control of any major council. For example, between 1922 and 1972 there was no Catholic mayor of the overwhelmingly Catholic city of Derry.

Unionist politicians therefore controlled all aspects of social and economic activity. They allocated the annual subvention from Westminster as they saw fit. They decided where public housing would be built and who would be housed in it. The vast but ailing engineering and shipbuilding industries, located mainly in east Belfast, which had formed the core of Unionist prosperity were naturally protected and provided with favourable commercial conditions. Jobs in these industries went overwhelmingly to Protestants.

When new industries, such as man-made fibres, textiles and chemicals, were encouraged to locate in the North in the 1960s they went to majority Protestant districts. Areas with Catholic majorities, like Derry city and county and counties Tyrone and Fermanagh, languished in rural poverty with huge unemployment figures. For forty years, from 1921, Northern Ireland really was, in the words of its first prime minister, Sir James Craig, governed by 'a Protestant parliament for a Protestant people'.

By the 1960s a new generation of Catholics had grown up after the Second World War. Thanks to the extension of the British free education system to Northern Ireland they were better educated than their parents and demanded a bigger role in society. They were not prepared to accept second-class status. They expected a fair society and demanded that the standards which applied in the United Kingdom as a whole should apply to the North of Ireland. They were ready to agitate to achieve these standards of justice and fair play, following the example and using the methods they saw others demonstrating elsewhere in the world. The Unionist administration in the North was equally determined not to allow the outside world in.

Despite their best efforts, Northern Ireland, it seemed, could not remain immune from the changes the 1960s brought to the world. Everywhere in the West young people who had grown up since the end of the Second World War wanted radical change. The signs were all around: television, The Beatles, topless swimsuits, President John F. Kennedy, a liberal pope, John XXIII, in the Vatican. These things affected the North as much as anywhere else. A fad for satire that ridiculed authority figures and derided the Establishment swept through Britain. This fad was exemplified by the magazine *Private Eye* and by the hard-hitting, disrespectful, topical TV programme 'That Was The Week That Was', which the BBC took off the air in the run-up to the British general election of 1964, so damaging was it considered to be to the Conservative government.

When the forty-nine-year-old O'Neill, an Anglo-Irish, Eton-educated former Irish Guards officer, replaced Brookeborough, he indicated his intention to change the ethos his predecessor had maintained. He talked about 'imaginative measures'. Most unionists assumed he was referring to modernising the North's flagging industrial economy, but it soon became apparent that he meant reaching out to the 35% Catholic minority who had been frozen out of the State. The Catholic community was growing rapidly. They were disaffected, they identified with the Republic of Ireland and withheld allegiance from the Unionist government, which existed to maintain the link with Britain.

O'Neill began to visit Catholic schools and was photographed shaking hands with Catholic clergy. Many unionists approved. The unionist evening newspaper, the *Belfast Telegraph*, endorsed the overtures. Unthinkably, even the tribal news-sheet of unionism, the *Belfast Newsletter*, oldest newspaper in Britain and Ireland (established in 1737), caught the mood. Its obituary of Pope John XXIII in June 1963 praised his reforms.

Others were not so taken with the new atmosphere. O'Neill was an awkward, remote man and a poor politician. He had prepared no one for his change of direction, least of all his Cabinet members who had happily supported Brookeborough's icy exclusion of northern nationalists. Within six months of taking office, O'Neill was the subject of a whispering campaign led by his most ambitious and able minister, Brian Faulkner, who alleged that his tentative reforms would open the floodgates to uncontrollable change.

In the wider unionist community there was also disquiet. Opposition to change was expressed most vociferously by Rev. Ian Paisley, a thirty-seven-year-old Protestant clergyman of prodigious physical proportions with a voice to match. Paisley's first appearance on the political stage had been fifteen years before when, at the age of twenty-two, he had campaigned in the 1949 Stormont election in the Dock constituency in Belfast. There he organised a ferociously sectarian campaign, which wrested the seat from Labour.

SHORT HISTORY OF THE TROUBLES

Paisley had established his own Free Presbyterian Church in 1951. His religious fundamentalism is a toxic mix of raw politics, anti-Catholicism and evangelicalism delivered at full wattage. In a five-decade career of implacable resistance to change, Paisley has always managed to rouse the darkest fears of the unionist community in the North.

He had embarrassed the Unionist government about marches and flags in the 1950s. In 1959 his threat to lead thousands of Belfast's Protestant shipyard workers to the small County Derry town of Dungiven and force a banned Orange Order march down the main street of the Catholic town led to the dismissal of the Unionist Minister of Home Affairs. Once again, in 1963, it was his direct street action to prevent change and his verbal assaults on Terence O'Neill that shot Paisley to prominence. His ability to connect religion and politics, combined with his incomparable flair for publicity stunts, made a volatile cocktail. An early sign of his power to stir up old hatreds was his protest march against an unprecedented gesture by Belfast City Hall when the Union Jack was lowered to half mast to mark the death of Pope John XXIII. Despite his march being banned, about 1,000 protesters joined him, waving Union Jacks.

Further evidence of Paisley's potential to provoke major trouble came in 1964 during the British general election campaign. One of the features of the Troubles has been that, by coincidence, British prime ministers have repeatedly called general elections at the most inauspicious moments for political developments in the North of Ireland, perhaps the most disastrous occasion being 1974 when groundbreaking new political arrangements were less than two months old (*see* page 43). October 1964 was the first such occasion.

The response of northern nationalists to prime minister O'Neill's liberalising gambit had not been one of gratitude. Far from it. A new wave of young Catholic professionals had emerged as a result of free university education. They saw O'Neill's promotion of change as an admission that their grievances were genuine. They wanted quick results. They began to publish statistics on injustices such as systematic discrimination in jobs and housing and electoral gerrymandering, which ensured majorities of Unionist councillors in towns where there were nationalist voting majorities. They made contact with sympathetic Labour MPs in Britain, many of whom had large contingents of Irish Catholics in their constituencies. They had, it seemed, found their voice, and they knew what they wanted to say.

DIVIS STREET RIOTS

It was in this climate that the British prime minister, Sir Alec Douglas-Home, called a general election. The election did not involve O'Neill's regional government, but would nevertheless be a revealing test of Unionist attitudes to his reform programme. Northern Ireland had twelve seats at Westminster: Unionists held them all. The only chance for nationalists was the West Belfast seat with its large, densely packed Catholic population.

When Paisley received information that an Irish tricolour was displayed in the window of the election office of the republican candidate, he announced his intention to lead a march into the heart of west Belfast to remove the flag. Rather than tackling Paisley, the police decided to remove the flag themselves. It was replaced, but when the police smashed the window and seized the second flag, the reaction was two days of the worst civil unrest since 1935: the Divis Street riots. Petrol bombs were thrown and police used water cannon. The disturbances galvanised the unionist electorate who poured out to vote and retain the seat.

The Divis Street riots displayed most of the ingredients which were to become standard fare over the following decades: the appeasement of Unionist extremists, like Paisley; the close connections between Unionist politicians and Northern Ireland's police force, the RUC, which was 90% Protestant; the RUC in riot gear, backed up by armoured cars, pitted against Catholic crowds; baton charges; running battles in the streets; petrol bombs. In 1964 only gunfire was absent.

The Divis Street riots were a shock, especially to young nationalists who had never seen the RUC in full paramilitary action. Nevertheless, the warning signs in west Belfast did not deflect any group from the course on which they had embarked. Catholic professionals strengthened their ties to MPs in prime minister Harold Wilson's newly elected Labour government in Britain in the hope of radical reform of Northern Ireland; various strands of Unionist opposition to reform began to join forces to conspire against Terence O'Neill; while O'Neill himself also ignored the Paisleyite message from Divis Street and quickened his pace.

In January 1965 O'Neill crossed his Rubicon when he met the Irish Republic's leader, Taoiseach Sean Lemass, in Stormont and returned the compliment by travelling to Dublin in February. No northern premier had met his southern counterpart since the 1920s. O'Neill had given no warning of the meetings, which critics bitterly denounced not only because Lemass had been prominent in the IRA during Ireland's War of Independence (1919–1921), but more importantly because all previous overtures from Dublin had been spurned while Articles 2 and 3 of the 1937 Irish Constitution remained in place: these Articles claimed the six northeastern counties as part of the national territory of Ireland. For Unionist hardliners, O'Neill's meetings with Lemass meant tacit acceptance of the hated Articles.

The fact that the Nationalist party at Stormont immediately responded to the O'Neill–Lemass meetings by accepting the role of official opposition at Stormont damaged O'Neill further in the eyes of his Unionist critics. To them, O'Neill's openness to change seemed merely to have whetted an insatiable Nationalist appetite. All his actions were construed as concessions to Nationalist demands. Even more alarming, prominent British Labour MPs were openly sympathetic to those Nationalist demands, which were carefully couched in the modern language of civil rights and equality rather than in traditional irredentist rhetoric.

O'Neill now faced the central problem which has confronted all his successors as Unionist leader. Could he reform fast enough to satisfy the nationalists whose hopes for change he had raised, yet slowly enough to placate the opponents of change within his own party and the wider unionist electorate?

Any illusions O'Neill had of a period of calm were dashed by extensive plans in the North to celebrate the fiftieth anniversary of the 1916 Easter Rising, plans which horrified unionists who had sought to expunge all Irish imagery from their State. O'Neill later said the anniversary soured the whole atmosphere. Northern nationalists took the opportunity to parade, displaying republican symbols officially endorsed by the Dublin government. Many rushed to buy a specially struck commemorative silver coin featuring an icon of Irish republicanism, Patrick Pearse. Right on cue, the British prime minister, Harold Wilson, called a general election ten days before Easter, timing certain to raise emotions to boiling point in the North.

In this election west Belfast's nationalist voters, determined not to waste the opportunity as they had in 1964, swung behind Gerry Fitt, a classic urban, working-class politician. He was elected amid tumultuous scenes. A former merchant seaman, Fitt was an experienced Belfast councillor and Stormont MP. He was sharp, articulate and combative. In debate he had a devastating line in repartee. He excelled on television. Unionists feared his tongue.

Fitt's victory in west Belfast marked a turning point. For the first time in decades there was a nationalist presence in Westminster. Advised and supported by veteran Labour MPs who instantly warmed to his working-class rhetoric, Fitt managed to overturn the convention which prevented questions about the North being asked at Westminster. He was able to bring nationalist grievances onto the floor of the House of Commons, to the intense discomfort of Unionists.

The fevered political mood of 1966, the Easter commemorations, Gerry Fitt's victory, the undisguised joy of nationalists, a hostile Labour government in Britain with a large majority – all helped to convince many on the wilder shores of unionism that Northern Ireland's existence was being threatened. A tiny group of men, less than a dozen, in the loyalist heartland of west Belfast, the Shankill district, styled themselves the Ulster Volunteer Force (UVF) after the militia established in 1913 to prevent Home Rule. They declared 'war' on the IRA. Within weeks of Easter they began a campaign of violence, attacking Catholic-owned property and, most seriously, killing two Catholics in gun attacks and an elderly

Protestant woman in a petrol bombing that 'went wrong'.

The IRA in 1966 was a figment of the UVF's imagination. For all practical purposes the IRA ceased to exist as an armed force after the failure of its 1956–1962 campaign. That series of attacks, also known as 'the border campaign', was desultory but deadly for all that. Organised from Dublin, the targets tended to be customs posts at the border with Northern Ireland, and RUC barracks in towns near the border. The campaign had largely petered out by 1958 due to internment of IRA suspects without trial both in the Republic and in the North. Even so, in 450 incidents eight IRA men and six RUC men were killed and thirty-two British soldiers injured. Damage to property, etc, in the North amounted to about stg£1 million.

After the collapse of the border campaign a new generation of men, based in Dublin, had emerged to lead the IRA. They had been attempting to divert the movement to a Marxist analysis of the northern problem. They concentrated on organising tenants' associations and infiltrating trade unions. They were moving into politics. But for ultra-loyalists like Paisley and the UVF, the IRA, red in tooth and claw, was a necessary bogeyman. Nonetheless, O'Neill acted against both Paisley and the UVF: he banned the UVF and Paisley went to prison in July 1966 for three months on his third conviction for unlawful assembly.

Even so, the Unionist prime minister was now in a cleft stick. Growing opposition to him within his own party required him to face down a heave against him in September, yet nationalists were complaining loudly that his talk of change was just that, mere rhetoric. They increased the pressure by organising a full-scale civil rights campaign.

CIVIL RIGHTS

By February 1967 the Northern Ireland Civil Rights Association (NICRA) had been formed, an umbrella covering people from organisations and political groups ranging from the Communist party to middle-class English academics at Queen's University, Belfast, to republicans, both Catholic and Protestant. They presented O'Neill with a list of six demands, including reform of the voting system for local government which gave businesses multiple votes. That gave them their powerful, though in twenty-first-century terms politically incorrect, slogan, 'One Man, One Vote'.

Faced with mounting dissent from Unionists, O'Neill dared not respond to nationalist politicians. Seeing republicans among the members of NICRA, senior Unionists accused the association of being an IRA front. That accusation made it impossible for O'Neill to deal with NICRA.

Led by educated, articulate young people, NICRA consciously modelled their movement on the contemporary black civil rights movement in the USA. In 1968 they began to organise 'civil rights' marches following the example of Martin Luther King, familiar then to everyone from television pictures. They sang the black civil rights anthem, 'We Shall Overcome'. One banner with 'Civil Rights' printed on it led their marches. The Unionist administration made all the same mistakes as the authorities in the USA's Deep South. They called NICRA members communists, republicans, IRA. They allowed the marches to be blocked by 'counter-marches', actually club-wielding gangs of thugs Ian Paisley organised to occupy the centres of towns NICRA planned to march in. They made the marchers look like victims and the forces of the State look like fascists.

In 1968 television had made all sides aware of the power of mass demonstrations with the huge anti-Vietnam War confrontation in Grosvenor Square, London, and *les évenements* in Paris which so badly rattled the government of General de Gaulle. Some members of NICRA deliberately sought to create the same kind of atmosphere in the North.

Finally, in October 1968, in full view of Irish television cameras, the RUC attacked a major civil rights march in Derry, injuring seventy-seven marchers and bystanders. Prominent among the marchers were Gerry Fitt MP and some English Labour MPs he had brought to the North with him. Fitt appeared on television, deliberately allowing blood from a baton wound on the head to pour down his face. The images flashed around the world. Irish-American politicians sat up and took notice. The British government was intensely embarrassed and annoyed at having to answer questions about events in Derry.

In very short order Terence O'Neill, accompanied by his main critics, Brian Faulkner and Bill Craig, the latter a hard-line minister who had praised the RUC for their behaviour in Derry, found themselves in Downing Street facing British prime minister Harold Wilson and home secretary Jim Callaghan. O'Neill was compelled to produce a reform programme largely comprising the demands of the civil rights movement. Both Faulkner and Craig strongly objected to the reforms, but O'Neill could not defy the British government. Could he defy his own party? And would his party defy the British as their grandfathers had done in 1912 when Ulster Unionists had imported rifles and ammunition from Germany and threatened to resist, by force of arms, British proposals for self-government, or Home Rule, in Ireland? Only time would tell.

2. Onto the Streets, 1969

Faced with serious dissent in his Cabinet and increasing turmoil on the streets, O'Neill went on local television in December 1968 to appeal for calm. O'Neill said Ulster stood at the crossroads, facing a choice. He asked prophetically:

> 'What kind of Ulster do you want? A happy and respected province, in good standing with the rest of the UK, or a place continually torn apart by riots and demonstrations, and regarded as a political outcast?'

It became known as the 'crossroads speech'. The answer to O'Neill's question came immediately. While NICRA with its moderate leadership was prepared to give O'Neill time to implement his reform package, others were not.

The People's Democracy (PD) was a loose grouping based at Queen's University in Belfast and dominated by radical students. Inspired by Trotskyist-led student movements prominent in street disturbances in France and Germany in 1968, the PD announced a plan for a 'long march' from Belfast to Derry, a one-hundred-and-twenty-kilometre trek over the New Year holiday period. Only about fifty diehard student supporters participated in the march, which most of them viewed as a sort of adventure.

Daily their route took them provocatively through some of the staunchest loyalist districts in rural Northern Ireland. Violence was inevitable; but when it came, on 4 January 1969 in an ambush at Burntollet bridge, an isolated spot amidst rolling green hills deep in County Derry, its scale and ferocity were shocking. Scores of loyalists, including off-duty members of the B Specials, armed with clubs and stacks of stones, ambushed the marchers. The RUC stood by as the attackers bloodied the marchers in fields, streams and ditches, belabouring male and female alike in full view of television cameras.

One response to the violence meted out to the PD march was more badly stewarded PD marches in other towns, including Newry, located on the southern border with the Irish Republic. There the march was accompanied by rioting and serious damage. The discipline of NICRA marches had been lost to PD-controlled street demonstrations.

Another response came from the British government. Aghast at the televised scenes of Burntollet and ensuing street violence, the British prime minister believed rapid reform was the solution. He publicly demanded it. Unionists believed reform was capitulation. O'Neill's administration began to totter. He had sacked Bill Craig, his most mutinous minister, in December, but in January Brian Faulkner, Minister of Commerce, resigned in protest at O'Neill's decision to establish a commission of inquiry into the 1968 disturbances. In February 1969, twelve Unionist MPs met and demanded O'Neill's resignation.

To try to stabilise his government O'Neill called a snap election, always a risky move in a crisis. The election result confirmed that the once rock-solid Ulster Unionist party had fissured. It showed that the UUP believed O'Neill himself was the issue: its candidates stood as 'pro-' and 'anti-O'Neill' Unionists. The division in Unionist ranks in the newly elected Stormont parliament meant that O'Neill did not command a majority for reform in his own party.

On the nationalist side there had also been striking change. Long-standing figures in the old, ineffectual Nationalist party were swept away. New, younger, better educated, more articulate MPs emerged from the civil rights movement, among them John Hume from Derry.

Bombs

There then followed an extraordinary series of events. In March and April 1969 bombs exploded at electricity sub-stations and major reservoirs which supplied over 60% of Belfast's water. The RUC naturally assumed the IRA was to blame. O'Neill called up 1,000 B Specials to guard such installations.

In the midst of this bombing campaign a rancorous by-election for the Mid-Ulster Westminster seat was being fought. Bernadette Devlin, a final-year psychology student at Queen's University and a prominent figure in the PD, won in a 92% poll. She took her seat at Westminster on her twenty-second birthday and, defying tradition – which requires a new MP to wait a few respectful weeks before making a non-contentious speech – made her maiden speech an hour later. And what a speech it was. She was instantly famous for her fluent, comprehensive, penetrating dissection of Northern Ireland and its Unionist regime. Her speech was published in papers all over Ireland and Britain. Every newspaper and TV programme wanted an interview. Jim Callaghan, the home secretary, acclaimed her brilliance. A prominent Conservative MP, Norman St John Stevas, said it was the 'most electrifying' maiden speech for forty years. Tiny, waif-like, quick-witted, alert, superb on TV, a child of the 1960s, Bernadette Devlin was a nightmare for Unionists, who appeared like clodhoppers compared with her.

Her election win and rapturous reception at Westminster were more hammer-blows to unionism.

Despite the public and private pressure from Harold Wilson, the reaction of the majority of Unionists was to dig in their heels and resist change. It turned out that this reactionary sentiment lay behind the series of explosions which had caused most people to believe another IRA campaign had begun. The truth was that the UVF had detonated the bombs, a fact which only became apparent six months later, in October 1969, when a bomb exploded prematurely at Ballyshannon power station, County Donegal, killing the UVF man who was planting it. (He had helpfully printed 'UVF' on the lining of his coat.)

The motive behind the bombing campaign was to undermine O'Neill and halt his reform programme by making it appear that the IRA was threatening Northern Ireland's existence. At least Unionists knew how to deal with that familiar threat, whereas they were at a loss as to how to cope with the demands for equality embodied in the civil rights campaign.

The UVF plot worked perfectly. The bombs, the disruption of water and electricity supplies, coming on top of regular disturbances in towns across the North, led to O'Neill's resignation on 28 April 1969, ten days after Bernadette Devlin's election and, by coincidence, the day she made her maiden speech. O'Neill himself said later in his memoirs that the bombs 'quite literally blew me out of office'.

In unionist districts joy was unconfined; celebratory bonfires blazed in the loyalist Shankill. On 1 May, Major James Chichester-Clark was elected UUP leader by one vote over Brian Faulkner. The only difference in the candidates' positions was who would oppose reform more rigidly. To this day some unionists blame O'Neill for opening a breach in Fortress Ulster. With touching naïvety many unionists believed the problem had gone away with O'Neill. Chichester-Clark – from the landed aristocracy, well-meaning, of plainly limited intelligence, devoid of ideas – was not the sort of man to rock any boat, let alone steer it. To draw a line under the dreadful period just past he declared an amnesty for anyone charged or convicted for offences committed since October 1968, which wiped the slate clean both for Derry's riots and for Burntollet bridge.

It was all wishful thinking. Immediately the twin pressures of reform and reaction started to squeeze the new prime minister. NICRA announced a civil disobedience campaign, and Chichester-Clark found himself and Brian Faulkner, now Minister for Development, in Downing Street agreeing that there would be 'one man, one vote' in local government elections. Westminster quickened the pace of reform, reducing the North's seventy-three local councils to seventeen, and its councillors from 1,200 to 400, changes certain to end Unionists' iron grip on every parish pump. At the same time NICRA renewed its marches, demanding that the rest of its reform programme be implemented.

All this as the so-called mad month of July approached, the month when unionists celebrate the 1690 victory of Protestant King William of Orange over Catholic King James II at the River Boyne in County Meath, a victory that inaugurated centuries of Protestant Ascendancy in Ireland. Each year in the North of Ireland marches by the Orange Order, a society set up in 1795 to extol the virtues of Protestant Ascendancy, cause public disorder as they pass through, or close to Catholic districts. The period from June to September each year, with up to 3,000 marches, not surprisingly is known as 'the marching season'.

The 1969 marching season would be doubly dangerous because, to the fury of Orangemen, civil rights marches as well as Orange marches were going to proceed in many locations. Even if they had wished to, the North's 3,500 policemen and women could not have effectively controlled events on the streets.

GUNFIRE

Matters came to a head in Derry on 12 August as thousands of loyalists from all over the North paraded through the overwhelmingly nationalist city. The marchers belonged to an organisation called the Apprentice Boys of Derry, which annually commemorates the start of the Siege of Derry in 1688 when apprentices shut the walled city's gates against King James II's army. In 1969 the marchers were neither boys nor apprentices, and only a fraction were from Derry. Derry's nationalist youths and loyalist marchers threw stones at each other. The RUC, heavily outnumbered, tried to force local stone-throwers back into the Catholic district known as the Bogside.

Quickly the confrontation escalated. The RUC baton-charged. The rioters halted them with a rain of petrol bombs. Fighting went on into the night and next day. The RUC fired CS tear gas into the narrow streets of the Bogside, its first use in Ireland or Britain, but could not breach the hastily thrown up barricades. The events became known as the Battle of the Bogside.

Some civil rights figures appealed for demonstrations in other parts of the North 'to take the heat off Derry', a dangerously naïve appeal, because when crowds came out on the streets in a number of nationalist towns, but fatally in west Belfast, many unionists interpreted their appearance as part of a coordinated insurrection.

Very serious rioting broke out in west Belfast on 14 August as police tried to quell demonstrations in support of the people of the Bogside. Shooting broke out and the RUC decided to use armoured cars with high-velocity 0.5in-calibre Browning heavy machine-guns mounted in turrets. Police fired this powerful armament in bursts, bullets tearing through the walls of high-rise flats in the nationalist Falls Road district to kill a sleeping nine-year-old boy.

As police baton-charged mobs in the Catholic district, hordes of Protestants followed behind the police, invading streets off the Falls Road and burning the homes of Catholics. There were similar scenes in the nationalist Ardoyne district in north Belfast. Thousands of people in west and north Belfast fought in streets lit by flames from blazing houses.

On 15 August British Army troops were deployed on the streets of west and north Belfast, as they had been in Derry's Bogside the day before. The British soldiers arrived amid scenes of jubilation from the beleaguered Catholics. People hailed them as saviours from the wrath of the RUC and the B Specials. The RUC was withdrawn. A generation later the RUC still remained unacceptable as a police force in those areas.

Harold Wilson's government set up a tribunal of inquiry into the riots under Mr Justice Scarman, who reported that ten people were shot dead, 154 wounded by gunfire and 745 injured. Scarman found that 83% of premises damaged were occupied by Catholics and that of 1,800 families displaced, 1,500 were Catholic.

These cataclysmic events had many permanent results. The

first was the construction of so-called 'peacelines' by the British soldiers, initially rudimentary barriers of wood and barbed wire to keep nationalist and unionist communities in Belfast and Derry apart. These barriers proliferated and over decades grew into six-metre-high concrete, and ten-metre-high chain mesh walls as polarisation intensified all over west and north Belfast.

Another consequence which has proved enduring was the emergence of a revitalised IRA to defend Catholic districts from a repeat of the depredations that had taken place in August 1969, sometimes with the connivance of the RUC. The worst example had been in Bombay Street, west Belfast, where loyalists had burnt houses under the noses of armed RUC men. A graffito later proclaimed, 'Out of the ashes of Bombay Street rose the Provisional IRA'.

The widespread disturbances of the summer brought to a head growing discontent within the IRA, a movement that in the Belfast of 1969 could muster fewer than sixty activists with about half-a-dozen old guns. Some Belfast IRA men had been unhappy about the Marxist direction their leadership in Dublin had been taking. The failure of the IRA to defend Catholic districts in August 1969 because the military side of the organisation had been run down was used by the traditionalists to discredit the Marxist-leaning leaders. Those opposed to the leadership, a minority in 1969, broke away and called themselves the Provisional IRA, so named because they intended to settle the issue finally at a convention in 1970, but the title stuck.

Intimate involvement by the British government in the affairs of the North became another permanent feature as a result of the explosion of violence in August 1969. Two senior British civil servants arrived in Stormont to direct reforms, the most urgent of which was to be a complete restructuring of the RUC and the abolition of the B Special militia. By October an affable English policeman, the former Commissioner of the Metropolitan Police, Sir Arthur Young, was charged with reorganising the RUC. In effect, the British home secretary, Jim Callaghan, was running Northern Ireland.

Loyalists vented their fury at these rapid, radical changes, particularly at what they considered to be the emasculation of 'their' security forces. There was serious rioting in loyalist Belfast during which, with terrible irony, the first RUC man killed in the Troubles was shot by UVF men who were rioting in defence of the RUC and the B Specials.

During the rioting that night two civilians were shot dead by the British Army, whose presence on the streets of the North of Ireland was to be the most enduring image of the Troubles. People in Derry and in Catholic parts of Belfast had welcomed the troops with jubilation as saviours from a pogrom. Many nationalists thought the soldiers' arrival signalled the end of Stormont and Unionist rule; so too did some unionists.

They were both wrong. The Army was deployed 'in aid of the civil power', as the official phrase had it. That civil power was the administration at Stormont and the aim of that administration was to get its own police force, the RUC, back in control as soon as possible. The British Army was to be Stormont's instrument for quelling what the now hard-line Unionist regime believed was a rebellion. It would not be long before the nationalists' welcome for the soldiers turned to bitter hostility.

3. Mayhem, 1969–1972

The deceptive calm which had spread over the streets of Belfast and Derry following the deployment of the British Army soon broke. Behind the barricades of nationalist districts, called 'No-Go Areas' because police and Army did not patrol there, the new IRA was organising under the leadership of veterans of the 1956–1962 campaign, including Joe Cahill.

These men understood immediately that the role of the British Army was to support the Stormont regime, which they believed to have been on the verge of collapse in August 1969. The emergent IRA held to the traditional republican view that Stormont was illegitimate and irreformable. Their response to the reforms the British government urged on the Unionist administration was: 'Damn your concessions; give us back our country.' The IRA set out to overthrow Stormont and to bring the British government to negotiate terms of a withdrawal from Ireland.

Soon riots, gunfire and explosions became common in parts of Belfast, notably in Ballymurphy where the twenty-two-year-old Gerry Adams lived, but also in Derry, on the edge of the Bogside where nineteen-year-old Martin McGuinness was prominent. Trouble then spread to other nationalist districts of the North, like Newry, Coalisland in east Tyrone, and Strabane on the Donegal border. In June 1970, during serious rioting in Belfast and Derry, the British Army shot dead five men as gun battles raged with hundreds of shots fired.

Political attitudes hardened in direct proportion to the violence. Nothing illustrates the shift in unionist sentiment better than two

Stormont by-elections in neighbouring constituencies in April 1970, caused by the retirement of the reforming Terence O'Neill and one of his strongest supporters. In a supreme irony, voters in O'Neill's former constituency elected the arch-opponent of reform, Rev. Ian Paisley, to Stormont. In the other constituency, a Paisley acolyte, Rev. William Beattie, was elected. In June, in a British general election, Paisley won the North Antrim Westminster seat, which he has held ever since. The warning for reforming Unionists was stark.

The two communities in the North were polarising sharply. With the intensification of the IRA campaign, an increase in UVF violence, the rejection by the unionist electorate of candidates supporting reform and the return of a Conservative government in Britain, the scene was set for the most violent years of the Troubles.

A MILITARY SOLUTION

The new Conservative home secretary, Reggie Maudling, a clever, lazy, corrupt politician, presented a sharp contrast to his Labour predecessor, Jim Callaghan. Maudling had no interest in Northern Ireland and no commitment to reform. He is famous for two remarks which perfectly sum up his attitude to the North. As his aeroplane took off from Belfast after one of his fruitless visits he called the flight attendant over: 'What a bloody awful country. For God's sake bring me a large Scotch.' Secondly, as the security situation deteriorated during his time in office he coined the phrase 'an acceptable level of violence', apparently conceding that there would never be stability in the North.

The new Conservative government, elected in June 1970,

brought a marked change in emphasis to British policy in the North. First, for historical reasons Conservatives supported the unionist position of maintaining the constitutional link to Britain, whereas many Labour politicians were sympathetic to the ideal of a united Ireland. Second, the Conservative party, whose official title was the Conservative and Unionist party, naturally had always maintained closer relations with Unionists than the Labour party had. Unionist MPs at Westminster sat on the Conservative benches and Unionists on the whole tended to support Conservative policies.

Third – and in the context of a burgeoning IRA campaign perhaps the most important change in the approach of the new government – was the decision to prioritise security by giving a greater role to the British Army and to soft-pedal reform. The net effect was that under the influence of Unionist ministers at Stormont, Army commanders had a freer hand on the streets. The consequences were disastrous. The most serious mistakes the British Army made occurred in the years 1970–1972 when they were acting at the behest of Unionist ministers.

Mindful of the fate of Terence O'Neill, Unionist leaders chased the chimera of defeating the IRA. They reverted to the old certainties, convincing themselves that the whole civil rights campaign had been a front for an IRA rebellion now exposed, and that the traditional measures of repression directed indiscriminately against the Catholic community would bring that rebellion to an end. In 1970 they had a sympathetic British government and at their disposal on the streets a heavily reinforced British military garrison, combined advantages no Stormont regime had ever enjoyed before.

Immediately they put these resources to use. A fortnight after the Conservative victory, on 3 July, the British Army, acting beyond their powers, imposed without warning what proved to be an illegal curfew for thirty-four hours on the whole Lower Falls area of west Belfast. Confining 20,000 people, including thousands of children, to their homes, soldiers began 5,000 house-to-house searches. Many homes were ransacked, much damage caused, many possessions wantonly destroyed and many looted by troops. The British Army killed four men, three of whom were shot dead and one crushed by an armoured car. None had any connection with the IRA.

The British Army never regained the trust of northern nationalists. Nine months after being welcomed as liberators, troops were spat at and stoned whenever they appeared in nationalist streets. In Belfast, recruits crowded into the IRA.

People throughout Ireland were horrified. One result of the 'Falls curfew' was an unprecedented visit by the Irish Minister for Foreign Affairs, Dr Patrick Hillery. Unannounced, and to the intense annoyance of both Stormont and London, he toured the Falls district the day after the curfew ended. His visit was an important sign that the northern Troubles were an issue in the politics of the Irish Republic.

Less than two months earlier the Taoiseach, Jack Lynch, had sacked two ministers, Charles Haughey, Minister for Finance, and Neil Blaney, Minister for Agriculture, as allegations emerged of attempts to import weapons destined for northern nationalists. The ministers were arrested and charged with conspiracy. The row threatened to split the ruling Fianna Fáil party, which prided itself on being the heir to the republican tradition of 1916. The trial and subsequent acquittal of Haughey and Blaney caused perhaps the most incendiary political crisis in the Irish Republic since the State's foundation. Some of its embers glow even today; as recently as May 2003 libel damages were awarded to one of the players in the crisis.

It was in this context that Dr Hillery visited west Belfast, to show solidarity with the people there and to demonstrate to supporters in the Republic that Fianna Fáil still laid claim to the Six Counties of the North. The very public anger of unionists did Jack Lynch and Patrick Hillery no harm at all in their battle for the soul of Fianna Fáil. On another level, Hillery's visit illustrated that the treatment of the nationalist minority in the North by the British was a matter that any Irish government ignored at its electoral peril. Repeatedly over the next thirty years actions by British security forces in the North, over which Dublin had no influence, would have serious political results in the Republic. There would be several such occasions in the two years following the Falls curfew.

Political survival may have been the spur for the actions of Jack Lynch's government, but in the North politics were pushed aside. Civil rights leaders who had been elected to Stormont came together in August 1970 under the leadership of West Belfast MP Gerry Fitt to form the Social Democratic and Labour party (SDLP). The SDLP was strongly in favour of participating in the North's institutions provided they were radically reformed to permit equal treatment of both communities. The party accepted that there could be no change in the constitutional position of Northern Ireland without the consent of a majority there. It was the first time since the foundation of the State that the political representatives of the nationalist community had adopted such policies.

The former Nationalist party, which the SDLP displaced, had been ambivalent about participation in the North while Sinn Féin, the political mouthpiece of the IRA, refused to recognise the existence of Northern Ireland, abstained from all institutions and supported the use of violence to expel British forces from Ireland. With the appearance of the SDLP, northern nationalists for the first time had a modern party with a recognisable political orientation, namely social democratic, prepared to operate at every level in the North. Unfortunately, in 1970 their voices of moderation went unheard amid the din of riots, explosions and gunfire. Events on the streets had the initiative.

By September the IRA and UVF had detonated one hundred explosions since the start of the year. Twenty-one people had been killed, among them constables Samuel Donaldson and Robert Millar near Crossmaglen, the first RUC men the IRA killed in the Troubles. Although prime minister Chichester-Clark pressed on doggedly with reforms agreed in 1969, they had no effect on the violence. For the IRA, reforms to Stormont counted for nothing. They wanted rid of Stormont. They stepped up their campaign.

By early 1971 there was daily rioting in parts of Belfast and on the margins of the Bogside district of Derry. British soldiers were in the front line, regularly firing the new rubber bullets, CS tear gas and now, fatally, live rounds at people they claimed threw petrol bombs and nail bombs. In Belfast, in February, the IRA shot dead the first British soldier to die in the Troubles. The British government had begun to hint at abolishing Stormont.

INTERNMENT WITHOUT TRIAL

Exhausted and out of his depth, Chichester-Clark resigned on 20 March 1971. Three days later Brian Faulkner at last achieved his ambition when the Ulster Unionist party made him prime minister. He would be the last man to hold that office. Faulkner was under no illusions about his task: he had to bring the streets under control or Stormont would go. He tried a mixture of stern security measures and what was for Unionists radical political reform.

Faulkner moved quickly to offer the SDLP chairmanships of powerful new committees at Stormont – the first time nationalists had ever been given any role in running the North. While the SDLP was considering the offer, violence once again overtook political developments. During days of sustained and intense rioting in Derry, the British Army shot dead two men whom witnesses claimed were innocent. When demands for an inquiry were rejected, John Hume, a Stormont MP for Derry, persuaded the SDLP to withdraw from Stormont and set up its own alternative assembly, a gimcrack gathering known as the 'Dungiven Parliament' from its location in the small County Derry town. Its short-lived existence was symbolic of the sharpening division in northern society.

With his political initiative rebuffed, Faulkner concentrated on the security side of his plans. There had been a steep escalation in violence in 1971. To add to the continual rioting, now shootings and bombings had become daily occurrences. Faulkner was struggling to persuade the British government that internment of republican suspects without trial was the only solution.

He had used this measure when he was Minister of Home

Affairs in the 1950s and believed it had defeated the IRA's so-called border campaign of 1956–1962. There were three major differences in 1971: first, the Irish government was not about to introduce internment as they had during the border campaign, therefore the 1970s IRA could flee across the border; second, there had only been dozens in the IRA in the border campaign, whereas in 1971 there were over 1,000 in the IRA's Belfast brigade alone; third, most of the IRA membership was new, young and unknown to RUC intelligence, the Special Branch.

Nevertheless Faulkner got his way, despite the misgivings of the General Officer Commanding Northern Ireland, Harry Tuzo. It was a desperate last throw, on the understanding that if it failed the British would set aside Faulkner's government and Stormont. On 9 August, in an exercise code-named Operation Demetrius, the British Army interned 342 men; all but one of those was Catholic. It would be February 1973 before any loyalist terrorist suspects were interned, even though by that time the UVF and UDA had murdered over one hundred Catholics.

Operation Demetrius was a disastrous failure in every respect. Ferocious gunfights and extensive rioting erupted in Catholic districts. Thirteen people were killed on the day of internment. Within two days one-third of the internees had been released, having no connection with the IRA. Hundreds of Catholics fled to the Republic as refugees. The whole Catholic population of the North was in uproar. When it became known, in October 1971, that British soldiers and RUC men had tortured selected internees with beatings, sleep deprivation, incessant so-called white noise and starvation diet, the anger and disgust of northern nationalists knew no bounds. As one, they withdrew their consent from the State. Rent and rate strikes began. Violence soared. In 1970 twenty-nine people were killed; in 1971 an incredible 180 died, of whom ninety-four were civilians.

As the death toll mounted towards the end of the year it was clear that Faulkner's last throw had failed. Parts of Northern Ireland were out of control. Huge gun battles raged between soldiers and the IRA in republican areas. The government responded by increasing troop numbers, adopting a more punitive policy towards rioters and a more aggressive military posture towards the IRA. The result was more deaths on all sides. Violence was increasing exponentially.

The turning point came in Derry on Sunday, 30 January 1972 when a civil rights march was stopped at an Army barricade. What had become daily, ritual stone-throwing at troops began, but on this occasion the usual Derry garrison had been supplemented by soldiers from the Parachute Regiment, already notorious for their brutality in Belfast. For reasons never satisfactorily explained and still being investigated, the paratroopers opened fire on the unarmed crowd and killed thirteen people. Another died later and seventeen were injured by gunfire.

The outrage had an electrifying effect on the whole of Ireland. The British ambassador to Dublin, Sir John Peck, wrote in his memoirs that it '... had unleashed a wave of fury and exasperation the like of which I had never encountered in my life, in Egypt, or Cyprus, or anywhere else.' Dublin recalled its ambassador from London. A day of national mourning was declared in Ireland. A crowd estimated at 35,000 marched to the British embassy in Dublin and burned it down. The IRA could not cope with the flood of recruits as young men and women queued to join.

Bloody Sunday, as the events in Derry came to be known, sealed the fate of Stormont. London had to take responsibility for security in the North, particularly as more and more British troops poured in to deal with the surge in violence which the killings in Derry had provoked. On 24 March, following a period of horrendous violence, the British prime minister, Ted Heath, announced direct rule from Westminster after Brian Faulkner refused to yield control over law-and-order powers.

DIRECT RULE

For Unionists the abolition of Stormont was a huge defeat and a profound shock, made worse by the jubilation exhibited in nationalist quarters and the triumphalism of the IRA, which took the credit. Brian Faulkner and Bill Craig appeared on the balcony at Stormont to speak in forlorn bitterness to an immense funereal protest rally of perhaps 100,000 unionists. Faulkner told the crowd their parliament was gone, but that:

> 'Northern Ireland is not a coconut colony and nobody and no coconut commission will be able to muster any credibility or standing.'

Other unionists had already opted for direct action. Shocked by the fierce IRA resistance to internment, working-class loyalists in Belfast formed the Ulster Defence Association (UDA) in August 1971; by the end of 1972 it would have 40,000 members. By the time Stormont fell the UDA was busy with its own terror campaign, convinced that the security forces were not being tough enough with republicans. Not content with shootings and bomb attacks in mirror image of the IRA campaign, the UDA began to stage fascist-style marches through Belfast, with thousands of masked men wearing motley army-surplus camouflage outfits. The authorities made no attempt to stop them. The two communities were at daggers drawn.

It was in these grim circumstances that the first secretary of state for Northern Ireland took office. Instead of the panoply of Cabinet and parliament, one English politician was to be responsible for running Northern Ireland. The first incumbent was Willie Whitelaw, a highly experienced Conservative politician, able, clever, patrician, yet gregarious and popular. Dubbed 'Willie Whitewash' by Ian Paisley, unionists regarded him with deep suspicion. What further humiliations had he in mind? Everyone was in unknown territory.

Whitelaw immediately set to work to find some political route out of the morass into which Northern Ireland had sunk. His first aim was to end the violence. To this end he put out feelers to the IRA to try to arrange a ceasefire. With leading members of the SDLP acting as go-betweens, a truce was agreed on 26 June 1972. Ten days later, on 7 July, Whitelaw secretly met IRA leaders, including Gerry Adams and Martin McGuinness, in London.

The meeting was a fiasco. The IRA delegation, led by chief-of-staff Seán MacStiofáin, made impossible, peremptory demands, including a British withdrawal from Ireland, to be completed by 1 January 1975, and an immediate amnesty for all political prisoners, internees and all those on 'wanted' lists. Whitelaw and his advisers concluded they could not do business with the IRA. Two days later the truce collapsed in an exchange of gunfire in west Belfast, amid recriminations between the IRA and the British Army.

There then followed weeks of ferocious bombing and shooting, culminating in what came to be called Bloody Friday in Belfast on 21 July when twenty-two bombs exploded, killing eleven people and injuring 130 others, many critically. With over 20,000 troops in the North the British administration decided to put an end to the barricaded No-Go Areas in Belfast and Derry where the IRA had a free hand to organise such coordinated attacks. On 31 July, in Operation Motorman, the Army entered the No-Go Areas and established patrol bases there. Violence continued unabated.

Undaunted, Whitelaw got down to a serious consideration of the political options open to him. By September he was ready to discuss these options at a conference of northern political parties in Darlington, England. A month later, on 30 October, he published a discussion paper on the political future of the North.

This document contained two basic tenets which have remained constants of British policy. One, Northern Ireland would remain part of the UK until a majority voted otherwise, but there would be no return to majority rule. Two, Britain also accepted that there needed to be recognition of what Whitelaw called 'an Irish dimension' to any settlement in the North.

Many of Whitelaw's actions had dismayed unionists and caused deep hostility among some: his meeting with the IRA, which had become public; his granting of Special Category Status to republican prisoners; his discussions with the Irish government. As a result, some Unionists boycotted his Darlington conference. These concerns were manifested at the extreme end of loyalism by UDA violence against innocent Catholics, which had surged dramatically with numerous, random sectarian murders.

The year ended in a paroxysm of violence north and south as

UVF bombs exploded in Dublin in December, killing two men and injuring 127 others. It was the worst year of the Troubles and the most violent year in Ireland since 1921, with almost one hundred dead in July alone. In total, 497 people died in 1972 in hundreds of explosions and over 10,000 shooting incidents.

4. False Dawn, 1972–1976

Labouring throughout 1972 in the shadow of relentless bombing and murder, Willie Whitelaw and his team of officials rapidly worked up a skeleton of what they considered a rational and reasonable system of administering the North of Ireland. After consulting Faulkner's Unionists and Gerry Fitt's SDLP and, for the first time since 1921, involving the Irish government in these discussions, Whitelaw produced plans in March 1973 which remain the essentials of British policy to this day.

He proposed an assembly elected by proportional representation. Members would elect an executive of ministers from both unionist and nationalist communities. The executive would be linked to the Irish government through a Council of Ireland made up of ministers from north and south, an idea resurrected from the Anglo-Irish Treaty of 1921, which established the Irish Free State. Whitelaw announced elections to a northern assembly in June 1973, after which delegations from Northern Ireland parties would enter negotiations with the Irish and British governments to forge the nuts and bolts of his scheme, called 'power-sharing with an Irish dimension'.

That, at any rate, was the timetable that Whitelaw drove along with admirable skill and determination. The northern secretary faced problems on two fronts. First was widespread opposition among unionists. Most of them resisted the idea of sharing power in an administration with nationalists. On top of that, unionists were horrified by the proposed Council of Ireland and the powers vested in it, which they regarded as a slippery slope to 'Dublin rule'.

Second, the IRA vehemently opposed any arrangement that included a northern assembly, or retained a role for Britain in Irish affairs. Republicans believed the proposals Whitelaw set out were designed merely to stabilise Northern Ireland and copper-fasten partition. Provisional Sinn Féin, which had been established as the political wing of the newly created Provisional IRA in 1970, and in 1973 was very much the IRA's junior partner in the republican movement, naturally continued the republican policy of boycotting all Stormont elections. They did not recognise the partition of Ireland and repudiated any role for Britain on the island. As for the IRA, they vowed to destroy any institutions emerging from elections.

Despite such opposition Whitelaw pressed ahead to try to construct a moderate centrist coalition comprising the nationalist SDLP and Brian Faulkner's Unionists. By the end of 1973 he appeared to have succeeded, but the truth was that the unionist community was deeply divided and Brian Faulkner was unable to retain the support of a majority in his community.

The history of the next three years, 1973–1976, indeed some would say the next thirty years, is one of repeated attempts by British secretaries of state to find enough Unionists willing to share power with nationalists in an assembly. Each attempt resulted in more fissures in Unionist politics, and more moderates being driven out of Unionist politics.

In 1973 British hopes rested on Brian Faulkner, the man who had worked so hard to undermine Terence O'Neill. After the events of 1971–1972, Faulkner had realised that the only way he would ever run Northern Ireland again would be to accept British government policy, which required changes infinitely more radical than those he had castigated O'Neill for advocating. Still, among unionists Faulkner possessed the inestimable advantage of being thoroughly disliked and distrusted by nationalists, most particularly because of his introduction of internment in 1971. It was hoped his reputation as a hardliner would encourage unionists to trust that the Union with Britain was safe in his hands.

Initially, it seemed as though Faulkner would be able to deliver the goods. His thirst for power not yet slaked, he supported Whitelaw's controversial proposals and led a sharply divided party into assembly elections in June 1973: a party so divided that some of his own election candidates opposed his policy. Although Faulkner's UUP remained the largest party, he failed to win the support of an overall majority of unionists in the election. Even so, he persevered and entered negotiations with the SDLP and the Irish and British governments, negotiations which culminated in December at a civil service training school called Sunningdale in Berkshire, which gave its name to the power-sharing agreement signed there.

Sunningdale was historic for a number of reasons, not least because for the first time it treated both communities in the North as equals. Gerry Fitt, for the SDLP, and Brian Faulkner, for the Ulster Unionists, both signed the Agreement as such. Hitherto the Unionist government of the North had always been regarded as the sole voice speaking for all inhabitants. Never again.

It was also the first Agreement about constitutional matters affecting Ireland signed by both the British and Irish governments since partition in 1921 – Edward Heath, the British prime minister, and Liam Cosgrave, the Irish Taoiseach, being the joint signatories in 1973. Following Sunningdale the Irish government was joint signatory of all Agreements on the North.

When the final details of the Sunningdale Agreement became public, it was pretty much as Whitelaw had proposed at the outset: an executive of ministers from both communities sharing power and those ministers sitting on a Council of Ireland with ministers from the Irish government in Dublin. Faulkner had not prepared anyone in his party for such a leap of faith.

He faced intense opposition within his own party from leading figures like former junior minister John Taylor. Almost 50% of the 860-strong Ulster Unionist Council (UUC), the ruling body of Faulkner's UUP, were opposed. The majority of Unionists in the assembly – made up of the Democratic Unionist party (DUP) led by Ian Paisley, the Vanguard Unionist party (VUP) set up by former minister Bill Craig after the collapse of Stormont, and individuals linked to loyalist terrorist groups – were, of course, also opposed.

For the Ulster Unionist party, sharing power with nationalists was bad enough, but a Council of Ireland was a step too far. On 4 January 1974 the UUC, aghast at Sunningdale's plans to involve Dublin ministers in the North's affairs, defeated Faulkner on the issue of a Council of Ireland. On 7 January he resigned as Ulster Unionist party leader, to be replaced by Harry West, a stolid County Fermanagh farmer in whom the predominantly rural UUC members had confidence as a traditional unionist, resolutely opposed to any fancy new ideas.

Nevertheless, Faulkner, now leading a minority rump of the UUP, forged ahead to form a power-sharing executive with himself as chief minister and the SDLP's Gerry Fitt as deputy. His own group's votes combined with those of the SDLP would enable Faulkner to struggle on against the majority of Unionists.

It was a high-risk, provocative strategy. The sight of prominent figures from the civil rights movement, like Gerry Fitt and John Hume, as ministers, people many unionists blamed for all their woes, led to scuffles in Stormont and noisy protests as the new ministers tried to carry out their duties. The only hope seemed to be that if the executive provided good administration over a period of time people would become reconciled to it. Time was not available.

Once again internal British politics impinged on events in the North of Ireland. Prime minister Ted Heath faced a crisis as industrial unrest in Britain reached a climax with a miners' strike. In February 1974, Heath called a general election on the question, 'Who governs Britain?' The resounding answer was, 'Not you, mate.'

In the North the question was different. There, the election was a referendum on Sunningdale – the last thing the two-month-old power-sharing executive needed. For its opponents the election was a Godsend. Harry West's UUP, Ian Paisley's DUP and Bill Craig's VUP came together to fight the election under the umbrella of the United Ulster Unionist Council (UUUC). With the slogan, 'Dublin is just a Sunningdale away', they won eleven of the twelve Northern Ireland Westminster seats and 51% of the total vote. Gerry Fitt was the only pro-Sunningdale MP returned.

It was a fatal blow to the Sunningdale Agreement. Among Unionists the UUUC victory destroyed any claims to legitimacy made by the power-sharing executive. Yet to their fury, Faulkner and his minority Unionists ignored the British general election result and pressed on regardless, in combination with the SDLP.

INSURRECTION

It was into this fraught political scene that Harold Wilson, once again prime minister, sent Merlyn Rees as northern secretary. Rees proved to be one of the weakest and most indecisive secretaries of state ever appointed to the North. An SDLP minister, Paddy Devlin, said he didn't mind Rees wrestling with his conscience: the problem was the result was always a draw.

Within a month of his arrival in March 1974, Rees faced nothing less than an insurrection by the unionist population of the North against British policy, an insurrection which illustrated what was wrong with the North. Leaders of the UUUC sat with leaders of loyalist terrorist groups, like the UVF and the UDA, and conspired to bring Northern Ireland to a standstill. The front organisation, which led what Unionists called a 'constitutional stoppage', had the curiously Bolshevik-sounding name the Ulster Workers' Council (UWC), despite containing men with extreme right-wing political views.

On 14 May the power-sharing executive won a vote of confidence in the assembly. Immediately the UWC swung into action, or rather inaction. Unionists demonstrated their exclusive control of Northern Ireland: they literally had their hands on all the levers of power. Workers at the main power stations cut generating capacity and industry began to grind to a halt. Workers at the giant Harland & Wolff shipyard and Shorts aero-engineering factory downed tools. The UDA controlled distribution of oil by road tanker from the North's single refinery.

There was widespread intimidation at roadblocks run by UDA gangs in the greater Belfast area, but the fact was that the majority of the unionist population acquiesced in the stoppage. Officials from Britain were shocked at the complicity of senior civil servants, police and ordinary workers in the strike. Within days electricity was rationed. The UWC was in control of petrol and food supplies over most of the area east of the River Bann. Devoid of political direction from Rees, the British Army was powerless. Yet even if soldiers had broken up roadblocks – and they made no attempt to do so – the Army had no engineers who could man the power stations. Within a fortnight the power-sharing executive collapsed after the inevitable resignation of its Unionist ministers, led by Brian Faulkner.

Nationalists were shocked, frightened and outraged. The UWC strike had been accompanied by a wave of sectarian murders, some directed against Catholics who had tried to carry on business during the strike. The sight of police standing at roadblocks chatting to club-wielding UDA thugs confirmed nationalists' worst fears about the nature of the State. They observed the impotence of the British Army with disbelief and were disgusted at the weak performance of the new secretary of state.

British government policy was in tatters. The majority of Unionists had decisively rejected proposals to share power with the nationalist community represented by the SDLP, but more ominously they had shown that they were prepared to defy the British government by supporting civil disobedience backed up by violence. Perversely, Unionists persisted in the belief that Sunningdale was a concession to republicans, despite the fact that the IRA castigated the SDLP as 'traitors to the Irish people' for their support of Sunningdale and had stepped up their armed struggle against the British plans. They were equally as determined as Unionists to prevent the Sunningdale Agreement from working, though for diametrically opposite reasons.

Sunningdale had been a false dawn. Far from being a solution it turned out not even to be the end of the beginning, as Churchill had described the first British successes in 1942 in the Second World War. It was time to step back and retrench. Perhaps Sunningdale had been too far, too fast in the aftermath of the horrendous bloodletting of 1972. Merlyn Rees announced in July 1974 that there would be elections to a 'constitutional convention' where northern politicians would have the chance to hammer out their own solution to the conundrum of running the region.

Following the failure of their meeting with the IRA in 1972 the British had simply excluded republicans from the political equation and had tried to establish political institutions in the midst of continuing violence from both sides. They had failed. Now, in the summer of 1974, the British began to secretly put out feelers again to find a way to end the IRA campaign. There were similar overtures to the loyalist UVF.

DEAD-END

For months there was no evidence that any of these contacts was bearing fruit; the violence did not abate. The UVF was responsible for the highest one-day death toll of the Troubles when, on 17 May 1974, they detonated three huge car bombs in Dublin and another in Monaghan, killing thirty-three people and injuring hundreds. The IRA began a devastating campaign in England with explosions in Guildford, Surrey, in October which killed five people and injured fifty-four. In November, in one of the worst atrocities of the Troubles, IRA bombs in Birmingham pubs killed twenty-one people and injured 182.

Yet despite this carnage, agents acting behind the scenes on behalf of the British had managed to produce an indefinite ceasefire from the IRA, which came into effect in February 1975. Merlyn Rees allowed British officials to meet Sinn Féin, and in a further attempt to encourage republicans to take a political path, 'incident centres' run by Sinn Féin were established in republican districts with telex machines provided by the Northern Ireland Office and direct telephone lines to local British Army commanders. This facility would open a direct line of complaint for republicans about possible ceasefire breaches by British forces thereby, it was hoped, preventing potentially lethal misunderstandings. Similar moves were made on the loyalist side with the UVF no longer proscribed.

In May 1975 elections to the long-promised convention finally took place. The result was a foregone conclusion. UUUC candidates secured an overall majority in the convention. Since the UUUC parties were all opposed to power-sharing, there was no hope of any outcome satisfactory to the SDLP or the British and Irish governments.

Negotiations away from the main floor of the convention failed by the autumn, and in October the convention, which had been tasked to produce administrative structures with 'the most widespread acceptance throughout the community', voted 42-31 in favour of a return to majority Unionist rule. The convention had failed.

By the end of the year there was absolutely nothing to show for all the political effort. The UVF had been banned again after a splurge of murders in one day in November when they killed eleven people. The IRA ceasefire had never been formally discontinued, but had long since disintegrated as individual units engaged in sporadic sectarian murder not admitted by the IRA. Catholic districts, particularly in Belfast, had been wracked by an internecine feud between the Official IRA and the Provisionals which caused many deaths. In November, Merlyn Rees closed the incident centres, a sure signal the British regarded the ceasefire as over.

By 1976 both the UUP and the political party Ian Paisley had formed, the Democratic Unionist party (DUP), were resolutely opposed to power-sharing. The British gave up on constitutional experiments and settled down to a long war of attrition against the IRA in the forlorn hope that if the IRA were defeated, Unionists might be prepared to share power with their nationalist fellow citizens.

Observers agreed that a resolution to the North's travails was further away than at any time since the violence began.

5. Retrenchment, 1976–1980

By the beginning of 1976 it was depressingly obvious that all sides in the conflict were settling in for a long haul. The IRA knew the aim which they had proclaimed in 1970 of driving the British out of the North in a frontal assault was a crazy dream. As for the British, three governments' political and security policies had failed. The IRA campaign against police and Army was as determined as ever, both IRA and loyalists were still at each others' throats, and the IRA campaign had extended to Britain itself. After seven years of uninterrupted violence, Northern Ireland was as unstable as ever with no resolution in sight.

Daily life in Northern Ireland had been utterly transformed by the IRA bombing campaign. Every sizeable town in the North and many smaller ones now had barriers manned by soldiers to prevent car bombs being driven in. The centres of larger places, like Belfast and Derry, were protected by so-called Gated Areas, comprising 2.5-metre-high fences with gates at all major entrances. Civilian 'searchers' frisked anyone entering through the gates. Within the Gated Areas all shops also employed searchers. Long queues formed at the gates and at the entrances to shops. In the early evening the gates were locked and the centres of Belfast and Derry became ghost towns. Outside the towns, random military vehicle checkpoints delayed travellers and disrupted business. People became resigned to the queues, the detours, the bomb scares, the increasingly intrusive security measures.

A Northern Ireland Office (NIO) publicity campaign of the time gives a flavour of the weariness. The slogan was, 'Seven years is enough'. Republicans countered effectively with the graffito, 'Seven hundred is too much', a reference to the republican claim of seven hundred years of British occupation. The NIO dumped their slogan. It was time for new strategies all round.

Although their policies had failed, the British government felt that their administration in the North of Ireland had weathered the storm. They had taken everything the IRA could throw at them and although the picture was bleak, violence had reached a plateau. They had learned from experience. If they were at a loss for a way out of the mess, at least they knew what didn't work. Trying to take the IRA head-on and wipe them out, the British now knew, was a non-starter. They had also learned the appalling impact of bad publicity in the USA and in the European Community, which they had joined, along with the Irish Republic, in 1973. Draconian measures against the nationalist population as a whole, along the lines of those the British had employed, admittedly unsuccessfully, to quell unrest in Africa and the Far East, were therefore out. Taking all these factors into account the British developed what came to be known as the policies of 'Ulsterisation' and 'criminalisation'.

Ulsterisation meant transferring as much of the security effort as possible to the RUC and to the locally recruited Ulster Defence Regiment (UDR), the successor of the B Special force abolished in 1969. Using locally recruited forces helped remove the image of a colonial war against a liberation movement, as the IRA had successfully portrayed themselves throughout the world.

The Ulsterisation policy had the added advantage of reducing what the British Army called 'infantry overstretch', namely the requirement to deploy large numbers of British troops in

Northern Ireland while NATO simultaneously required a large commitment at the Fulda Gap in West Germany. What was worse, men trained, in some cases at vast expense, to use tactical nuclear weapons in the event of a Soviet attack on West Germany were dying on the streets of west Belfast; better and cheaper to place locals in the forefront.

Finally, the policy aimed to deprive the IRA of the claim that they were fighting a war of any kind. Pushing the police to the forefront – 'police primacy' with the Army in aid, a scenario never the truth in the North's hot spots – allowed the British to present the North as a police emergency. To this end, the parallel policy of criminalisation was developed. The IRA were to be portrayed as simply a criminal conspiracy with no political content, a tiny minority with no support who would eventually be rounded up and jailed since the whole community was opposed to them, so the official line went.

A report in 1975 by an English judge, Lord Gardiner, had recommended the end of so-called Special Category Status for prisoners convicted of terrorist offences. That status had been introduced by Willie Whitelaw in 1972 as the price to end a hunger strike for political status by a senior Belfast IRA man. Special category prisoners enjoyed considerable privileges tantamount to prisoners-of-war, including being housed in compounds run by their own officers.

Internment was ended at Christmas 1975 and from 1 March 1976 anyone convicted of a terrorist offence would serve the sentence in the same conditions as other criminal convicts. A brand new jail had been built beside Long Kesh internment camp, sixteen kilometres outside Belfast, to house the expected influx of prisoners. It was designed as several jails within a jail, eight self-contained blocks, each in the shape of a 'H', all surrounded by a five-metre-high wall, three kilometres long, with sentry towers at intervals manned by armed troops.

The carefully constructed official position in 1976 was therefore that the North of Ireland was a society which did, admittedly, have many social and economic problems stemming from the past, but which was threatened by a criminal conspiracy directed by a small group of evil men. The government was determined to defeat this conspiracy.

A FAILING SOCIETY

That said, the British had also learnt that the North of Ireland was a very sick society indeed and that reforms in political structures would not solve its abnormal endemic problems. For a start there was systematic discrimination in employment and had been since before the origin of the State in 1921. Unemployment rates in Catholic districts were astronomical, up to 70% in the worst areas, such as Ballymurphy in west Belfast, or the Creggan in Derry, or Strabane in west Tyrone. In some families no man had been employed for three generations.

There is a story that in the mid-1970s, to test if unemployment was really that bad, one sceptical officer in the Royal Green Jackets sent his men out in Ballymurphy before dawn to record in their notebooks the number of men setting out for work. By 9.00am the senior NCO had brought the riflemen back, most with empty notebooks. There were about 6,000 adult males in Ballymurphy at that time.

Apart from black spots like Ballymurphy and the Creggan,

on average Catholics were almost three times as likely to be unemployed as Protestants. Traditionally Catholics had been excluded from skilled work in the engineering plants which had formed the backbone of the industrial prosperity of the northeast of Ireland since the nineteenth century. In the giant shipbuilding yards, notably Harland & Wolff, which employed 20,000 at its wartime peak, Catholics, if they got a job at all, had to make do with the unskilled and least secure work. When work was scarce, Catholics were first to be laid off. At times of political tension or crisis, Catholics were expelled from the premises, some literally running or swimming for their lives while being pelted with 7cm-long rivets known locally as Belfast confetti.

By the 1970s all that was history. Belfast's industrial glory days were gone forever, the shipyards and engineering works, like Mackie's in west Belfast, in terminal decline. But the legacy of unemployment among Catholics remained. On every scale Catholics came off worse, for example, in life expectancy, incidence of long-term illness and physical handicap. Only in education did Catholics excel; it was free, and there was no discrimination because the Catholic Church controlled Catholic education. It was the way out of the ghetto if you had brains.

In an attempt to address the running sore of the employment differential, the British administration in the North introduced the Fair Employment Act in December 1976 and established the Fair Employment Agency (FEA). The act made it unlawful to discriminate on grounds of religion, or political belief. Unfortunately, like much of the legislation the British passed, the NIO advice managed to emasculate it. Although it was to deal with one of the most corrosive issues afflicting the North, the FEA ended up with a budget one-tenth of that for the Arts Council for Northern Ireland, just over stg£250,000. That remained the case until the late 1980s when the involvement of the Irish government, with US support, brought about radical change in such matters.

Another example of useless legislation in the same period was the Incitement to Hatred Act 1970, designed to combat the sulphuric language which extremists in both communities hurled at each other. Advocates of the act hoped it would end the publication of scurrilous song books, chants and incendiary speeches by politicians and some self-styled Protestant clergy. Many hoped Paisley himself would fall foul of the act.

In the event, only one person has ever been successfully prosecuted under its terms, because for a conviction it is necessary to prove malice. George Seawright, a Glaswegian who became an ultra-loyalist Shankill councillor, was sentenced to three months and fined stg£100 in 1985 for advocating at a meeting of the Belfast Education and Library Board, of which, incredibly, he was a member, that Catholics and their priests be burned. He told the court he meant it because 'I am an honest bigot'. If he had not said that, he would have walked free. To this day there is still no effective anti-incitement legislation.

THE LONG WAR

While the British were beginning to wrestle with the responsibilities of developing policies for a long period of what came to be called Direct Rule, the Irish government, a Fine Gael/Labour coalition, had also been taking steps to prevent the seemingly interminable violence in the North from spilling over into the Republic. After the high point of Sunningdale, when the Irish government had been fully involved in the search for a settlement, the administration of Taoiseach Liam Cosgrave appeared to distance itself from the problems in the north of the country. The horrendous casualties caused by the Dublin and Monaghan bombs in May 1974 shocked and horrified Dublin politicians and made many disinclined to do anything which might result in more carnage in the south.

Increasingly the coalition government's policy on the North came to be dominated by Dr Conor Cruise O'Brien, one of the ministers from Labour, the junior coalition partner. O'Brien, an author and intellectual and an internationally known and respected figure from his work at the United Nations in the 1960s, became convinced that the real problem, not only for the North but for the whole of Ireland, was IRA insurgency and everything connected with it. He set out, as far as was in his power to do so, to destroy the republican movement. In his capacity as Minister for Posts and Telegraphs in 1976 he is best remembered for tightening the draconian Section 31 of the Broadcasting Authority Act, which banned republicans, or anyone believed to be supporting their aims, from the airwaves despite the fact that Provisional Sinn Féin was a legal political party.

As minister, O'Brien accused the Republic's national broadcaster, RTÉ, of allowing the IRA 'a spiritual occupation' of its portrayal of the North. He called Irish journalists 'political stooges'. His controversial amendment to Section 31 allowed RTÉ to ban any material which would 'tend to undermine the authority of the State'.

In line with O'Brien's analysis, the Irish government went out of its way to assure the British that everything possible was being done to rout the IRA and their sympathisers, so that there could be no suspicion of the Republic offering a safe haven to terrorists. Fine Gael, the dominant party in the coalition, had traditionally been strong on law and order and tougher on republicans than Fianna Fáil, the largest party in the Republic which had itself emerged from the republican movement in 1926.

As a result of the crackdown on republicans the Irish government was also accused by its political opponents of turning a blind eye to rough interrogation tactics employed by the Gardaí, the Irish police force, with republican suspects. It was alleged there was a special 'heavy gang' within the Gardaí who specialised in roughing up IRA suspects. In September 1976 the government went so far as to declare a state of emergency to enable it to take on extra powers, most controversially the power to hold suspects for seven days without charge.

Like the two governments, the IRA had also been busily redesigning their strategy. The initiative came in 1975 from inside Long Kesh, the internment camp the British renamed HM Prison Maze. A small group of prisoners, the most prominent of whom was Gerry Adams, re-thought the military and, more importantly for the long term, the political strategy of the republican movement.

They acknowledged that there would be no quick victory. They studied other conflicts in the world which they considered to be similar and came up with the strategy of 'the long war'. The IRA would wear the British down, sicken them with a ceaseless, remorseless struggle, so that eventually they would give up and leave. The days of big gun battles were over. There would be strategic bombing and tactical sniping – the 'war of the flea', as the title of one study of guerrilla warfare popular with republicans called such an approach.

The IRA would be reformed. Out went the old military units of brigade, battalion and company, which aped the structures of the British Army and were wide open to informers because everyone in the unit knew everyone else. Instead, there was to be a cellular system of Active Service Units (ASUs), each with four members. Crucially, the 'war' in the North was to be directed by a Northern Command made up of young men who had cut their guerrilla teeth in the early 1970s. Coincidentally, these young men began to plot within the IRA to push aside the older, mainly southern-based leadership who had no knowledge of conditions in what the IRA called the 'war zone', ie, the Six Counties, but mainly Belfast, Derry, Fermanagh, Tyrone and south Armagh.

The really novel development was the plan to build up Sinn Féin as a political organisation. Adams later wrote: 'If the struggle was limited to the armed struggle, once it stopped, the struggle stopped.' Without a political base there was no point having a ceasefire because there were no political structures to benefit from it. These conclusions emerged from bitter criticism of the ceasefire that the IRA leadership had called in 1975. As far as the northerners were concerned, there had been no results at all after a year on ceasefire except a weakening of the IRA. They resolved it would never happen again.

Thus, largely unknown to each other, by 1976 both republicans and British had laid down plans for a lengthy contest. It was to last twenty years. The full impact of the decisions taken by both sides in 1975–1976 did not emerge for a number of years. When it did, it fundamentally changed the nature of the conflict.

Prisons and Protests

In September 1976 the first IRA man convicted under the new regime, Kieran Nugent, entered HM Prison Maze, now better known as the H-blocks. He refused to wear the prison clothes issued to him; he said they would have to nail them to his back. Instead he wrapped himself in the blanket provided as bedding. He was the first 'blanket man'. Few in the outside world knew about him: in part because the British tried to keep secret the IRA's inevitable response to the removal of Special Category Status; in the main because in autumn 1976 Northern Ireland was dominated by the phenomenon known as the 'Peace People'.

In August, three west Belfast children were killed by a car careering out of control after British troops shot its IRA driver. Their mother was grievously injured. An aunt of the children, Mairead Corrigan, and a friend, Betty Williams, organised an impromptu march demanding, quite simply, peace. The response was astonishing. Thousands of people, mainly women, turned out. More marches along the Falls and Shankill roads led to a peace rally in Belfast of perhaps 20,000 people.

The Peace People made no conventional political demands. They simply demanded an end to violence, though of course that was a political demand. Nevertheless few saw it as such. The Peace People struck a chord. In November the two women won the Nobel Peace Prize. Then in 1977, as quickly as it had appeared on the scene, the bubble burst. The Peace People had never cut any ice with the political parties, and after an initial fright at the extent of the public outcry the IRA reviled them as tools of the British and continued their armed campaign uninterrupted.

Jim Callaghan, who had succeeded Harold Wilson as British

prime minister in April 1976, had appointed Roy Mason secretary of state, to replace Rees, in September 1976. Mason had seized eagerly on the Peace People as evidence to support the NIO's policy of criminalisation, but he overdid it. He rapidly became viewed as pro-unionist, revelling in tough statements about republicanism and forecasting the defeat of the IRA. He worked hard at 'normalisation', by which he meant bringing jobs to employment black spots. He tended to believe the North's problems were caused by massive unemployment and poverty, and if only the IRA could be crushed, then prosperity would solve the unrest.

In pursuit of that prosperity Mason is best remembered for granting a stg£56 million subsidy to American entrepreneur John De Lorean to develop and produce a space-age, stainless steel, gull-wing sports car in a purpose-built factory on the outskirts of west Belfast. The car didn't sell at the time, but has since become a collector's item, world-famous as the vehicle in the *Back to the Future* films starring Michael J. Fox. The project collapsed with millions of public money lost. At the beginning of this century the British government was still pursuing through the courts and arbitration the money Mason granted.

In the other track of his policy – crushing the IRA – Mason faced accusations, rather like his counterparts in the Republic, of giving the security forces a free hand against republicans and of turning a blind eye to human rights abuses. RUC interrogators routinely beat IRA suspects in a specially built interrogation centre at Castlereagh police barracks. Complaints by nationalist politicians, Catholic clergy, Amnesty International and police doctors about ill-treatment of suspects eventually led to an inquiry in 1978. Nevertheless, many men served lengthy sentences as a result of 'confessions' signed at Castlereagh. Often indeed Northern Ireland's special non-jury terrorist courts disgracefully accepted so-called unsigned confessions as the basis for conviction.

Mason was resolute in his rejection of all complaints and objections, but he was heaping up a huge mountain of resentment. One-hundred-and-fifty republican prisoners were 'on the blanket' by 1977, refusing visits except on rare occasions and then mainly as a pretext to pass messages to the outside. Partly because of assaults by prison warders during searches and while walking to and from visits, and partly because their 'blanket campaign' had got nowhere, in March 1978 IRA prisoners began to spread excrement around their cells. Their action became known as the 'dirty protest'. Again they got nowhere. Mason ignored them. He would grind them down.

There was some evidence to support the belief that he might. Violence had dropped off significantly in 1977 and continued at a reduced rate in 1978, even though horrific incidents continued to happen, the worst being the IRA firebomb in February at La Mon hotel outside Belfast, where twelve people were incinerated. Nevertheless, deaths were down to fifty-five from 220 in 1976 and never again reached the catastrophic levels of the early 1970s.

The reasons for this are debatable. Changing IRA tactics was certainly one explanation. A reduction in loyalist violence was another. Many people attribute this reduction to Roy Mason's defeat of a loyalist strike in May 1977 when Rev. Ian Paisley, with the help of the UDA, attempted a re-run of the 1974 UWC *putsch*. Mason's resolute crushing of the strike contrasted sharply with Merlyn Rees's dithering. Mason also benefited from the lessons the security forces had absorbed from 1974. Quick, sharp action by police and Army dispersed the first major roadblocks. Crucially, the power workers did not support Paisley this time and therefore there was no major public inconvenience.

Another important factor in the reduction in loyalist violence was the absence of any political initiative from Mason. There has always been a direct correlation between unionist violence and radical political proposals. Substantial sections of the unionist population always view political change as a threat, and some respond with violence, or the threat of violence. Combined with Mason's tough treatment of the IRA, his avoidance of any political challenge to unionism made unionists feel more secure than at any time since 1968. Even today they look back on Mason's period in office with some nostalgia.

In reality, it was the calm before the storm. By the summer of 1978 there were over 250 republican prisoners on the 'dirty protest'. The criminalisation policy was fundamentally flawed because the republican prisoners were not pariahs isolated from the Catholic community. On the contrary, conditions in the prisons were arousing serious concern in the Catholic community and further afield. The primate of all-Ireland, Cardinal Tomás Ó Fiaich, visited the Maze and said it reminded him of a Calcutta slum. Irish-American politicians were growing restive. International human rights bodies began to take an interest in the controversy. The IRA began to turn its attention to prison officers, who became targets for assassination; they killed ten in 1979, including the deputy governor of the Maze prison. Despite all, Roy Mason remained unmoved.

The Iron Lady

Any prospect of a resolution of the prison dispute receded over the horizon when a general election in May 1979 returned a Conservative government led by Margaret Thatcher. The new prime minister was instinctively sympathetic to unionism. Even had she not been, a series of what the IRA called 'spectaculars' in 1979 could only have hardened her attitude to republicans.

In March, two months before her election victory, her spokesman on Northern Ireland and likely next secretary of state, Airey Neave MP, was murdered by a republican splinter group, the Irish National Liberation Army (INLA). Neave had been Thatcher's mentor and confidant, the organiser of the campaign which brought her leadership of the Tory party. No sooner was she in office than there were two major IRA bomb attacks on the same day in August: one killed seventy-nine-year-old Lord Mountbatten, Queen Elizabeth's cousin, as he sailed off the coast of Sligo with members of his family; and two-hundred-and-forty kilometres away at Warrenpoint, County Down, eighteen soldiers, sixteen of them from the Parachute Regiment, were killed in a double bomb ambush. Thatcher immediately flew to Northern Ireland and announced an increase of 1,000 men to the RUC establishment.

Thatcher's priority was security. She set little store by political development, and who could blame her in 1979? The Rev. Ian Paisley's hardline DUP had won two seats from the UUP in that year's general election, and in the first European election in June, Paisley himself had topped the poll, making him the most popular Unionist politician in Northern Ireland. Attitudes had stiffened all round.

A visit to Ireland by the newly elected Pope John Paul II in September excluded Northern Ireland, partly because of vociferous objections by Paisley and the Orange Order, partly because of the continuing violence. During his visit, the closest the pope came to the border with Northern Ireland was Drogheda, a town eighty miles south of Belfast. There he made an impassioned plea, 'on bended knees', to the IRA 'to turn away from the paths of violence'. Three days later, on 2 October, the IRA rejected his plea, claimed they had widespread support and that only force would remove the British.

Few would have disagreed with Taoiseach Jack Lynch when he said, in November 1979, that the Northern Ireland problem 'continues to be as intractable as at any stage in the last ten years'. Few realised that the dispute simmering inside the prisons was about to produce an epic confrontation between the British government and the IRA, which would prove to be a watershed in the Troubles.

6. Hunger Strikes and Politics, 1980–1985

The years 1980–1985 were packed with some of the most dramatic developments of the Troubles: the deaths of ten republicans on hunger strike and the massive civil disturbances associated with those deaths; the emergence of Sinn Féin onto the political stage, with people formerly prominent in the IRA elected to public office; an almost-successful IRA attempt to wipe out the British Cabinet; major public stand-offs and slanging matches between Irish and British governments followed rapidly by the closest cooperation between the two governments since the foundation of the Irish State in 1921.

At the outset of her premiership, Margaret Thatcher followed what had become the well-worn practice of new administrations in Northern Ireland: a renewed crackdown on the IRA accompanied by the launch of the obligatory 'political initiative'. Her secretary of state, Humphrey Atkins, mild, incompetent, mediocre, was a person with whom it was difficult to associate the word 'initiative'. His efforts to set the political ball rolling again after four years of stasis under Mason were limited in the extreme and quickly ran into sand, but they nevertheless demonstrated the problem that would be a feature of the North's political scene for the next twenty-five years. It simply proved impossible to get all the parties around a table together.

Atkins's proposal was relatively harmless: to have a round-table conference involving the four main northern parties. The SDLP leader, Gerry Fitt – the party's only MP and, by 1979 spending more of his time at Westminster and becoming increasingly estranged from his party – was the only person who welcomed it. His party did not because the basis for discussion excluded the 'Irish dimension' introduced into northern politics by Whitelaw in 1972; neither was power-sharing a guaranteed outcome. Fitt resigned, though remained an MP. His more politically astute deputy, John Hume MEP, was elected SDLP leader in his place.

On the Unionist side, Ian Paisley simply refused to have anything to do with a conference, demanding instead the defeat of the IRA. James Molyneaux MP, who had succeeded Harry West in 1979 as UUP leader, also boycotted the affair. Molyneaux disliked any political initiatives, calling them 'high-wire acts'. He was content with direct rule and worked futilely to have Northern Ireland completely integrated into the UK. All the parties talked separately but inconsequentially to Atkins; he gave up in March 1980.

FIVE DEMANDS

March was also the fourth anniversary of the inauguration of the criminalisation policy in the North's jails. Republican resistance to the policy had been continuous and intensifying all that time, but commanded no support outside the republican community. It was not for the want of trying. Nationalist districts were festooned with H-block posters and banners. In the middle of main roads at rush hour people stood in Indian file in a 'white-line' protest, holding pictures of relatives 'on the blanket'. Protesters disrupted all kinds of public events.

A new feature was the appearance in republican areas of

immense lurid murals with quasi-religious overtones depicting prisoners in harrowing scenes from Castlereagh holding centre and dressed in blankets in H-block cells. Sometimes they clutched rosary beads in bony fingers. Hitherto murals had been the province of loyalists and had been mainly stylised gable-end paintings of King William of Orange on a white charger, which were touched up annually before the marching season. The need to keep the republican prisoners in the public mind changed all that as nationalists adapted the mural and made it their own. Since 1980 both republicans and loyalists have competed with each other in the production of murals, so much so that in recent years they have become recognised as an art form, the object of academic study and a means of tracing the changing political messages both groups wish to convey to their communities.

Despite all this energy expended on attracting public attention to the plight of prisoners 'on the blanket', there had been no breakthrough into public consciousness. The general public would not have been aware that by 1980 there were 837 republican prisoners in the Maze, over 300 of them on the 'dirty protest'. In February, thirty-two women in Armagh jail began their own dirty protest after male warders were used to quell a disturbance in their prison.

The prisoners had 'five demands' based around clothing, work and visits. If granted, they would amount to special status. Outside the jails their campaign was organised by the National H-block/ Armagh Committee. Some well-known figures, like Bernadette McAliskey, formerly the Mid-Ulster MP Bernadette Devlin, were prominent in the campaign, but it made no headway. Their failure did not prevent loyalists targeting them, and the UDA murdered some leading H-block activists. McAliskey herself was very seriously wounded in a murder attempt.

Inside the prisons frustration had been mounting, with some, including the IRA Officer Commanding (OC) Brendan Hughes, arguing for the use of republican prisoners' ultimate weapon: the hunger strike. For months the IRA's Army Council opposed the idea, partly because it would divert resources from their military campaign, partly because it might fail ignominiously. Finally, however, the Army Council gave in because the prisoners were going to do it anyway. They had tried everything else.

Seven prisoners, including Hughes, began a hunger strike on 27 October 1980. By 18 December one of the seven was critically ill in hospital and the NIO had apparently offered concessions on clothing. Hughes called off the strike. But the NIO offer was not what it had seemed. Too late, the prisoners decided the NIO had duped them. Early in 1981 a new OC, Bobby Sands – who had been elected to replace the exhausted and demoralised Hughes – began plans for another hunger strike, but instead of a group, it would be one man refusing food with another joining every week. If they had to die there would be a rolling series of deaths over months. Sands relinquished his position as OC in case his judgement failed him as death approached. He refused food on 1 March 1980, the fifth anniversary of the abolition of Special Category Status.

Four days later Frank Maguire, independent nationalist MP for Fermanagh–South Tyrone, died. James Molyneaux moved the writ for a by-election, hoping nationalist divisions in the constituency would yield a Unionist victory. It was a historic miscalculation.

Republicans hit on the idea of putting up Bobby Sands as a

candidate, some believing that the British government would not allow an MP to die, others realising that even if Sands were not elected the campaign offered an opportunity for huge publicity for the prisoners' plight, so conspicuously absent since 1976. Either way, a substantial vote for Sands would refute the British claim that he was not a political prisoner. In the highly emotive atmosphere surrounding the election campaign the SDLP stood aside and gave Sands a free run on the nationalist side. He won in a 92% poll: 30,492 votes to 29,046 votes for former UUP leader Harry West.

Sands's victory transformed the terms of trade in politics in Ireland. Since 1969 republicans had boycotted elections in the North of Ireland for ideological reasons, but also because they feared their armed struggle might be rejected by nationalists at the polls. Now they knew different. Following Sands's win, elections north and south were on the republican agenda.

In the short term, however, Sands's victory made no difference. Despite representations from all over the world to yield to the prisoners' demands, Mrs Thatcher would not relent. Sands died on 5 May. If his election had not done so, then his funeral – attended by 100,000 people and televised worldwide – demolished the British argument that he was not a political prisoner.

Three more hunger-strikers died at intervals in May, as planned, and so the deaths punctuated the summer months with huge funerals and frenzied rioting, until the hunger strike was called off in October with ten men dead. It petered out because prisoners' next-of-kin had begun to intervene when a hunger-striker lapsed into a coma: the families would not let any more die. It seemed a demoralising defeat, but the hunger strike was the watershed of the Troubles. Its ramifications were enormous.

At the time however, republicans concentrated on street protests during the period the men were dying, but especially immediately after each death. The result was unprecedented rioting in republican districts across the North, particularly in Belfast and Derry. There had been riots as intense in the 1970s, but never so widespread and prolonged; some lasted five or six days at a time. In Belfast alone British troops fired over 25,000 plastic bullets in 1981, killing and seriously injuring many people, including children not involved in any riot.

ANGLO-IRISHRY

The result of this unrest was that the two communities polarised to an extent never before imagined possible. That over 30,000 people, virtually the whole Catholic electorate of Fermanagh–South Tyrone, would vote for a convicted IRA man was a profound shock to many unionists. The fact that virtually every nationalist and Catholic public figure in Ireland had argued for some compromise with the hunger-strikers confirmed unionists in their belief that the whole nationalist community sympathised with the IRA. For their part unionists backed Mrs Thatcher to the hilt. They agreed with her that any deal with the hunger-strikers would mean a victory for the IRA.

Unionists also had other reasons to be concerned. Something political was going on above their heads and they didn't like the sound of it. When it had become plain by 1976 that there was no Unionist party prepared to share power with nationalists and that therefore there could not be devolved government in the North only unending instability, the Irish government had begun, from 1979, to explore the possibility of acting jointly with the British government on issues of mutual concern about the North. It was the beginning of a fundamental shift in the relations between Dublin and London, one which would ultimately form the basis of both the Anglo-Irish Agreement in 1985 and the Good Friday Agreement in 1998.

At the Fianna Fáil *árd fheis* in February 1980 the Taoiseach, Charles Haughey, who had succeeded Jack Lynch in December 1979, went public on this policy for the first time. In May 1980 he met Thatcher in Downing Street to discuss Anglo-Irish relations and presented her with an Irish Georgian silver teapot. The phrase 'teapot diplomacy' was coined, but it was the phrase 'the totality of relationships' in the communiqué which produced consternation among Unionists. That meant the British were discussing *them* with the dreaded Haughey in their absence.

A second, very high-powered summit convened in Dublin in December 1980. Thatcher, accompanied by foreign secretary Lord Carrington, the chancellor of the exchequer Sir Geoffrey Howe and the northern secretary Humphrey Atkins met with Haughey and senior Irish ministers. They announced joint studies to examine areas of cooperation, like economics and security. Haughey proclaimed the summit 'a historic breakthrough'.

Unionists were deeply suspicious, first because they automatically rejected any Dublin involvement in the North's affairs, but particularly because the whole project appeared to be driven by Charles Haughey, a real unionist hate figure. Many unionists blamed Haughey for the re-establishment of the IRA in 1970 and set no store by his acquittal in the Arms Trial of that year. Ian Paisley referred to the Taoiseach disparagingly as 'the son of an IRA gunman from Swatragh' – the nationalist town in County

Derry where Haughey's father came from.

Paisley launched a campaign against the Anglo-Irish talks in February 1981. His worst fears seemed justified when, in March 1981, Brian Lenihan TD, Haughey's Minister for Foreign Affairs, preposterously claimed that the Anglo-Irish talks could produce Irish unity within a decade. A Paisley rally in response brought 30,000 to Stormont, an indication of just how fevered the atmosphere in the North was even before Sands's hunger strike began.

Paisley need not have worried. Mrs Thatcher was furious at Haughey and Lenihan for overselling her meetings with them, and when she next encountered Haughey one witness described her as being incoherent with rage, barely able to speak. Another says she launched into a diatribe about the misrepresentations.

Soon both Thatcher and the Unionists were rid of Haughey for he was defeated in an Irish general election in June 1981. Flushed with Sands's success in Fermanagh– South Tyrone, hunger-strikers had stood in a number of constituencies in the Republic. Two were elected and others took sufficient votes from Haughey's Fianna Fáil to deprive the party of a majority in the Dáil. A Fine Gael/Labour coalition led by Dr Garret FitzGerald came to power. Haughey never forgave Thatcher, blaming her mishandling of the hunger strike for his loss of office.

By the end of 1981 it seemed to many that republicans had suffered a major setback: ten men dead but no political status. When the hunger strike ended, Jim Prior, who had replaced Atkins as northern secretary in September, gave the prisoners pretty well what they had been asking for in their 'five demands' about visits and clothes, but no alteration in their legal status. It looked like a magnanimous gesture from a victor. Mrs Thatcher said the IRA had played what might be 'their last card'. Anyone who knew Ireland realised the opposite was the case. The SDLP leader John Hume responded that, on the contrary, Mrs Thatcher had dealt the IRA 'a full deck'.

Jim Prior then proceeded to deal republicans some new cards. Like every northern secretary before him, Prior embarked on his inevitable political initiative. He called it 'rolling devolution', intending to give more power to northern parties the more they cooperated. He faced strong opposition not only from Mrs Thatcher, who had exiled him to the North because he was a heavyweight opponent within her Cabinet, but also from the Irish government and all shades of opinion in Northern Ireland. Despite these bad omens Prior determined to have assembly elections in 1982 to an assembly where he hoped all the main parties would be represented.

Nationalists and the Irish government were opposed to his plans because they marked a retreat from the principle of power-sharing and also because they cut across the joint governmental approach Dublin and the SDLP had favoured since 1979. After much dithering the SDLP decided to fight the elections but to boycott Prior's assembly, where power-sharing would be in the gift of Unionists.

Support for the SDLP

The SDLP was in poor shape in 1982. The party had been pushed aside in two hunger-strike by-elections in Fermanagh/South Tyrone, its representations on the hunger strike had been publicly rebuffed by Mrs Thatcher, and Sinn Féin had emerged as a real electoral rival whose strength grew in proportion to Thatcher's intransigence. After Sinn Féin's successes at the polls in 1981, their publicity director, Danny Morrison, had famously asked at the party's *árd fheis* in October that year, 'Will anyone here object if, with a ballot box in one hand and an Armalite in the other, we take power in Ireland?'

The SDLP had fought many elections but always against Unionists, never before within the nationalist community: since republicans abstained, it had simply been a matter of setting out a stall and collecting votes. Not any more. Sinn Féin had scores of volunteers fired with enthusiasm for 'the cause' and for the novelty of electioneering. In contrast, the SDLP looked old and tired, four of its six founding members had fallen by the wayside and other prominent figures had dropped out, demoralised after a decade without political progress. There had been no political forum since 1976; the party's only paid politician was its leader, John Hume. Now the SDLP faced an election where their abstentionist stance was indistinguishable from the real abstentionists: Sinn Féin.

Nonetheless, the SDLP did manage to hold its own in the assembly elections in October 1982. Overall, Sinn Féin got 10% of the vote compared to the SDLP's 18.8%, though Sinn Féin trounced the SDLP in some urban districts. The following year Sinn Féin's onward march continued in a British general election, the party's share of the vote rising to 13.4% compared to the SDLP's 17.9%. More than percentages was the symbolic importance of Sinn Féin winning over 100,000 votes in 1983 and its leader, Gerry Adams, defeating the SDLP's former leader Gerry Fitt in west Belfast, where Fitt had been MP since his historic victory in 1966. The governments in Dublin and London were shocked. The Irish government decided they must ride to the rescue of the SDLP.

There were a number of reasons for the Irish government's anxiety, not least the concern that if Sinn Féin sustained its rate of growth it would overtake the SDLP as the largest nationalist party in the North. Since Sinn Féin gave 'unambiguous support' to the IRA's armed struggle, no British government would engage in any political development with them. Furthermore, there was the potential for destabilising politics in the Republic of Ireland, as had happened in 1981 when thousands had voted for IRA hunger-strikers in northern prisons and thereby affected the result of the Republic's election. The endless violence in the North was also damaging the Irish economy, its tourism industry and its ability to attract foreign investment.

The Taoiseach, Garret FitzGerald, the most cerebral of all Irish taoisigh, set out to negotiate a new settlement in the North with the British which would end the growing alienation of northern nationalists, the reason, he believed, for the rise in support for Sinn Féin. Simply calling on the British to withdraw from the North, as Charles Haughey was doing as late as February 1983, was not a policy, rather it was a slogan that the British could ignore. Instead, FitzGerald set up the New Ireland Forum in May 1983 to hammer out an agreed position among the political parties in Ireland and then present it to the British government as the basis for negotiation. Sinn Féin was excluded because of its support for violence, but all other parties on the island were invited, though of course the Unionists ignored the Forum.

The New Ireland Forum was a 'leg-up' for the SDLP. The Forum sat in public, its members had access to officials from the

Irish government, to Leinster House where the Irish Parliament (Dáil Éireann) sits, and they were paid expenses. It was much more than a public relations exercise however, because in May 1984 it published its report, the first-ever considered analysis by an Irish government of the problem in the North and its effect on Ireland as a whole. It offered a set of three options which were to form the basis of the agreed negotiating position of all the nationalist parties in Ireland except Sinn Féin: a unitary state; a federal/confederal state; or joint authority over the North by Ireland and Britain.

The debating and compiling of the *Forum Report* had been a difficult and challenging exercise because of political and personal rivalries within and between northern and southern parties. Charles Haughey's Fianna Fáil held out for the unitary state as the 'preferred option' of the Irish government. Haughey, concerned at the political kudos his bitter rival FitzGerald would gain if negotiations were successful, hoped that the insertion of the unitary state option would put the kibosh on talks with the British. To strengthen his hand he had managed to exploit divisions within the SDLP between its leader, John Hume, and his deputy, Seamus Mallon, who was close to Haughey at the time. As it turned out, clever drafting by Irish officials and careful briefing from the same people made it clear to the British that FitzGerald's real preference was for joint authority over the North by Dublin and London.

'OUT, OUT, OUT'

To many the whole exercise seemed a forlorn effort to offer the trappings of a political platform to the SDLP as an alternative to the violence which dominated political life in the North.

Since the end of the hunger strikes the IRA had redoubled its activities, relying on huge bombs and landmines to kill members of the security forces as well as sniping in built-up areas. They also renewed their bombing campaign in England, some of the worst incidents being bombs which killed eleven soldiers in army bands in London in July 1982, and an explosion at Harrods department store in London during Christmas shopping in December 1983, which killed five and injured eighty people.

For their part the security forces seemed to have taken the view that with 40% of the nationalist electorate voting Sinn Féin, it was pointless trying to win the hearts and minds of any nationalists. In a series of violent incidents in 1982 members of a secretive RUC unit, E4A, killed six unarmed IRA and INLA suspects at road-checks in highly dubious circumstances which became known as the 'shoot-to-kill' incidents. An inquiry into the affair conducted by John Stalker, deputy chief constable of Greater Manchester Police, ended controversially when Stalker was suspended. His inquiry, continued by another senior English police officer, was never published. To this day inquests on those deaths have not been completed.

The security situation did not improve in 1984. In March, Gerry Adams was shot several times in a UDA attack, but survived. Seventy-two people were killed that year, including five in a devastating IRA attack in October on the Grand Hotel, Brighton, where the Conservative party conference was being held. Cabinet members were seriously injured and Mrs Thatcher herself narrowly missed the blast from the 25lb bomb, which tore a dramatic gash in the centre of the hotel's ornate façade.

In such conditions the New Ireland Forum's proposals for

negotiations between Ireland and Britain appeared forlorn indeed when Garret FitzGerald met Mrs Thatcher a month later. The outcome seemed to confirm the low expectations. At a press conference following a meeting with FitzGerald, Thatcher listed the three Irish proposed options and dismissed each with the phrase, 'That is out.' It became known as the 'Out, out, out' meeting.

FitzGerald records in his memoirs his deep dejection at this public relations disaster. But that was all it was. To outward appearance it looked as though all the work of the Forum had gone up in smoke at that meeting. The truth was quite the opposite. Two teams of officials, one in the British Cabinet Office with some Foreign Office officials, the other in the Irish Department of Foreign Affairs and Taoiseach's Office, had developed a rapport during the period since the publication of the *Forum* Report in summer 1984. They continued their work, under the direction of Mrs Thatcher and Garret FitzGerald, with the aim of producing an agreed Anglo-Irish approach to the problems in the North. Thatcher's abrasive response had simply misled observers into thinking she had shut her mind to any change.

Quite the contrary. During 1985 rumours began to circulate that Dublin and London were about to reach an agreement. Unionists reacted with disbelief. How could Mrs Thatcher, the most conservative and unionist prime minister since Churchill, a woman the IRA had almost killed the year before, the woman who had withstood all threats and blandishments during the hunger strike, how could such a person make a deal over the heads of Ulster Unionists? Yet she did, partly because she believed she was securing Northern Ireland's position in the UK as the

Irish government formally accepted there could be no change in the North's constitution without the consent of a majority, and partly because she believed greater security cooperation with the Republic could end the IRA's campaign.

So it was that on 15 November 1985, at Hillsborough Castle outside Belfast, Mrs Thatcher countersigned the Anglo–Irish Agreement with Dr Garret FitzGerald while thousands of enraged Unionists, led by some of their MPs, protested outside the castle gates.

7. Ballots and Bombs, 1986–1992

The years immediately following the Anglo-Irish Agreement (AIA) were a time when the communities in the North of Ireland operated more than ever in two parallel political universes. Unionists could see nothing but the AIA. They threw everything into trying to overturn it, using every political and extra-political device that had worked in previous generations to defeat any development they did not control.

On the nationalist side, Sinn Féin – completely controlled after 1986 by a new generation of determined northerners – moved rapidly into the political arena, fighting every election and demanding unconditional talks with Britain, despite continuing IRA violence. The Sinn Féin leadership also worked simultaneously to develop a *rapprochement* with the SDLP, ostensibly to try to achieve a united nationalist position, but ultimately to overtake the SDLP as the voice of northern nationalists, a strategy that was a source of concern to many in both the Irish and British governments. Would closer relations between the two parties make a deal with Unionists easier, or impossible?

The Anglo-Irish Agreement had come as an immense shock to the Unionist psyche. Unionists experienced an intense feeling of betrayal and insecurity, accentuated by the secrecy in which the British had shrouded the negotiations. Unionists were aghast that Northern Ireland, their State, the place the British had given them in 1921 to enable them to secure their position in Ireland, had been the subject of negotiations with the Irish government, the very entity which officially laid claim to the territory of

Northern Ireland. That same Irish government was now to have a consultative role in running the North. Not only had all this been done without Unionists' consent, it had been done behind closed doors, with no input from them whatsoever. Yet the Taoiseach, Garret FitzGerald, had kept the SDLP fully briefed.

In reaction, Unionist politicians launched a massive campaign of opposition. Initially they enjoyed significant public support, but as years passed resistance became largely confined to the Unionist political class, which withdrew all cooperation from the political system. Unionist politicians refused even to talk to British ministers. They refused to engage in political discussions unless intergovernmental meetings under the auspices of the AIA were suspended. They maintained this position for five years until the two governments conceded in 1991.

The Irish and British governments and northern nationalists were nonplussed at what they saw as unionism's wildly disproportionate reaction because, as a matter of fact, the consultation machinery the AIA established amounted to much less than unionists had feared and certainly proved much less effective than nationalists had hoped.

The basic tenets of the Agreement were these. An Anglo-Irish Intergovernmental Council was set up and chaired jointly by Ireland's Minister for Foreign Affairs and Britain's northern secretary. This Council was serviced by a permanent secretariat based at Maryfield, an unprepossessing two-storey building near Holywood, on the outskirts of Belfast. It was surrounded by heavy security fencing and stood adjacent to one of the main British Army garrisons in the North, Palace Barracks, a location which proved prescient when unionist protesters launched furious attacks in the early months of the AIA.

Maryfield was staffed twenty-four hours a day by British and Irish officials, the idea being to provide a system whereby the SDLP could make complaints on behalf of nationalists to Irish officials about the British administration in the North and have those complaints raised instantly at a high level. In fact, by 1986 the SDLP was so weak on the ground in the most troubled areas that the Maryfield apparatus was chronically underused. Irish officials set up their own network of contacts in the North, which meant meeting members of the clergy, lawyers, business people and others in the community to hear their views and opinions on current issues.

The Agreement provided for the Irish government to put forward 'views and proposals' for consideration by the Council. These 'views and proposals' could be about political, security, or legal matters, and cross-border cooperation. The British side of the Council need not accept any of these views and proposals: more often than not they either rejected them or were so dilatory and half-hearted in implementing them as to render them nugatory.

Underlying the AIA was a carrot-and-stick approach towards Unionists. Irish government interference was the stick; devolution was the carrot. It was made clear that the way to reduce Irish government input into the North's affairs was to agree a devolved administration for the North. Any powers devolved would immediately cease to be a matter the Irish government could raise through Maryfield. So, either share power with nationalists or suffer increasing Dublin interference.

Unionists would have none of it. Jim Molyneaux and Ian Paisley had only found out in autumn 1985 that there was going to be an

Anglo-Irish Agreement, and even then only in very general terms what its provisions would be. Unionist shock when the deal was clinched in November 1985 was palpable, because the unionist community was totally unprepared. It was a public humiliation for Molyneaux who, despite leading eleven MPs, had been kept in the dark by the British government. The unionist community was convulsed. Although most knew nothing of what the AIA contained, the symbolism was enormous. The Irish government now had a role in running the North and Irish civil servants were ensconced outside Belfast. Dublin had a toe in the door.

The day after the Agreement was signed Unionists announced that all fifteen Unionist MPs would resign their seats and force by-elections on the issue of the AIA. A week after the AIA was signed an enormous unionist demonstration, numbering over 100,000 people from all over the North, took over the centre of Belfast. The rally, predominantly working-class but attended by many middle-class professionals and office workers, was addressed by Jim Molyneaux and Ian Paisley. Paisley gave a characteristic rabble-rousing speech, ending with a phrase which became the Unionist catch-cry for the next number of years: 'Ulster says NO!' He went on, roaring for good measure, 'We say Nevaar, Nevaar, Nevaar!'

Later, in a fearsome sermon at his vast Martyrs' Memorial church, Paisley called down the wrath of God on Mrs Thatcher. 'We pray this night that thou wouldst deal with the prime minister of our country. O God, in wrath take vengeance upon this wicked, treacherous lying woman. Take vengeance upon her O Lord, and grant that we shall see a demonstration of thy power.'

It was all to no avail. God proved indifferent to Paisley's incantations. In Westminster the Commons passed the Agreement by an overwhelming 473-47 vote; Mrs Thatcher making clear she would not yield to violence, or the threat of violence from unionists. Given her resolute resistance to republican violence it could not be otherwise, and unionists knew it. The Dáil passed the AIA 88-75, Fianna Fáil opposing it because the party leader, Charles Haughey, claimed it 'copper-fastened' partition.

The AIA presented Unionists with the problem that, unlike with the Sunningdale agreement, they had no target, no institution they could pull down or boycott. Their protests could not prevent the two sovereign governments meeting to arrange the North's affairs. By-elections, followed by the mixture of boycotting, threats, intimidation and the weapon which had succeeded in 1974, a strike, all ended in failure.

DIRECT ACTION

In the by-elections, which took place on 23 January 1986, the UUP lost the Newry–Armagh seat to the SDLP deputy leader Seamus Mallon; he has held it ever since. Unionists' next major protest, a strike to bring the North to a standstill (perversely called a 'day of action'), was held on 3 March and backfired badly. Although many workplaces closed and there were some power cuts and disruption of travel by roadblocks, it proved a damp squib. The security forces were well prepared and kept most main arteries open. The unionist middle-class stood aside from the strike, damaging the credibility of Unionist politicians calling for support for the day of action. As a result, those who did turn out on the streets looked thoroughly disreputable.

Minor violence, particularly against police officers attempting to dismantle roadblocks, embarrassed Unionist leaders openly linked by the strike with figures in the UDA and UVF, whose masked hoodlums manned the roadblocks and intimidated workers. The UDA publicly jeered Unionist MPs for being willing to use paramilitaries but unwilling to do any dirty work themselves. The secretary of state, Tom King, whom Thatcher had appointed a month before the Agreement, accused Unionist MPs of making common cause with people in paramilitary garb, an accusation the chief constable of the RUC later repeated.

Loyalist terrorist groups were especially incensed that the RUC frustrated their attempts to defeat the Agreement on the streets. Loyalists felt special antagonism towards police because they blamed them for enforcing the will of the Irish government through the Agreement. Graffiti in loyalist districts read, 'RUC paid in punts': the Irish currency until 2002.

Throughout 1986 the UDA and UVF, spurred on by the incendiary language of Unionist politicians, petrol-bombed the homes of police officers and stepped up sectarian attacks on Catholics living in or near loyalist areas. By May 1986, 368 members of the RUC and their families had been attacked in the six months since the signing of the AIA, fifty in April alone. Seventy-nine homes of Catholic families were firebombed in the same month. The Housing Executive dealt with 1,118 cases of intimidation in 1986.

Fierce rioting by loyalists continued through the summer, mainly associated with Orange Order marches and police attempts to re-route them from Catholic streets, particularly in Portadown. The only loyalist killed by a plastic bullet was shot on Easter Monday in Portadown as police and Army fired hundreds such bullets at loyalist rioters. In a sinister development, Paisleyites began to take over town centres at night in protest against the AIA. Carloads of men, some wearing balaclavas and carrying cudgels, would descend on small towns in the dead of night and walk the streets menacingly. The tactic culminated in an incursion across the border into the small town of Clontibret, County Monaghan, led by DUP deputy leader Peter Robinson MP, who was arrested by Gardaí. He paid IR£17,500 in fines and compensation after pleading guilty to unlawful assembly.

By the end of 1986 it was clear the Agreement would not be overturned. Thatcher visited Belfast at Christmas and restated her commitment to it. Nevertheless, although demonstrations and direct and indirect action had failed, no Unionist politician was in any way reconciled to the AIA, or showed any likelihood of ever being so.

Nationalists watched the Unionist turmoil with no little satisfaction but some trepidation. Would the British give in to Unionist protests? It was an article of faith among both SDLP and Sinn Féin that previous failures by British governments to stand up to them had led Unionists to believe they could destroy any political initiative by violence, or even the threat of violence. Would it happen again?

This time the British government stood firm, but Unionist opposition did have an effect. British ministers were taken aback by the scale and duration of their opposition and as a result were extremely reluctant to introduce any measures under the Agreement which would further exacerbate Unionist hostility. This reluctance undermined one of the reasons the Irish government had pressed for the AIA in the first place, namely to shore up the moderate SDLP position in the North. The British reneged even on some of the smallest details, such as ensuring that British Army patrols, in particular UDR units, were always accompanied by police escort. They also refused to establish three-judge courts on the model of the Republic's Special Criminal Court, a measure the Irish government had believed the British were committed to.

After two years there were few tangible results from the AIA for nationalists to point to besides Unionist rage. Sinn Féin, who opposed the AIA, were soon able to claim that only Unionists' furious reaction made the AIA seem more radical than it was; that in practice it made no difference to the lives of nationalists in the North.

Yet it did. It was more than just a huge morale boost. Although both governments soft-pedalled to calm Unionist fears, nevertheless regular meetings of Irish and British ministers became the norm. It was not joint authority as Unionists alleged, although Unionists were right in one respect: Irish government involvement in decision-making in the North on a daily basis was a landmark. It did influence policy. Dublin banked the gains of the AIA and successive Irish governments built on them. The two governments found it in both their interests to work ever closer together.

One of the major achievements to emerge from this close contact was a new, draconian Fair Employment Act, which came into operation in 1989 and was administered by a Fair Employment Commission, a souped-up and heavily funded improvement on the 1976 Fair Employment Agency. Department of Foreign Affairs officials in Dublin had judiciously used American political clout to lean on the British and had managed to defeat NIO objections. In the years after 1989 the employment differential between Catholics and Protestants in the North began to sink, although even today Catholics are almost twice as likely to be unemployed as Protestants.

The IRA AND SINN FÉIN

While the Unionist protest campaign dominated news headlines, behind the scenes radical new directions in nationalist politics were being explored. Gerry Adams had become MP for West Belfast in 1983 and later that year president of Sinn Féin. He and the northerners around him, like Martin McGuinness from Derry, OC IRA Northern Command, worked carefully and tirelessly for the next few years to eliminate one of the great taboos of republicanism: abstention from Dáil Éireann. It was the firm belief of young republicans that standing for elections in the Republic but promising to abstain from a parliament which 99.9% of the population of the Republic accepted was just plain silly.

Adams had to jettison the taboo without alienating the IRA militarists. At the 1986 Sinn Féin *árd fheis* Adams's view triumphed. Any Sinn Féin TDs elected thereafter would take their seats. The old guard split from Sinn Féin and formed Republican Sinn Féin, soon to vanish into political oblivion. Once this hurdle had been cleared republicans moved on several fronts under the northern leadership.

First, the dual strategy: they aimed to pick up as many votes as they could while continuing the IRA campaign. The more votes for Sinn Féin, the more support republicans could claim for their overall policy. IRA hawks were reassured by bombings being stepped up in 1987 as a British general election approached. One massive bomb, near the border, just over a kilometre north of the Carrickdale hotel on the main Dublin–Belfast road, killed

Northern Ireland's second most senior judge, Lord Justice Gibson, and his wife.

When, in November 1987, French forces intercepted a coaster, the *Eksund*, carrying one-hundred-and-fifty tonnes of weapons and *matériel* from Colonel Gadaffi's Libya destined for the IRA, it emerged that IRA anxiety about running down the campaign had been well catered for. Three previous shipments had been delivered in 1985–1986, amounting to about one-hundred-and-twenty tonnes of weaponry and explosives, including the powerful Czech-made plastic explosive Semtex, which was to form the core of the enormous bombs the IRA used to devastate town centres for the next decade.

The IRA was therefore tooled up to continue its war indefinitely, a fact which assuaged the militarists. However, the thinking of the republican leadership was more complex. They planned to use the Libyan arsenal to demonstrate the IRA's capacity for unending violence, while at the same time trying to get into talks with the British without an IRA ceasefire. Northerners were convinced the 1975 ceasefire without guaranteed talks had been a fundamental mistake: that the British had just strung the IRA along. By 1986 the republican leadership believed that while force alone could not drive the British out of Ireland, only force could bring them to the negotiating table.

Second, in what developed into the most important and fruitful front, Adams also secretly put out feelers to the Irish government and the SDLP through a confidant, Fr Alec Reid, a Redemptorist priest at Clonard monastery in west Belfast. Sinn Féin also published an election manifesto, *A Scenario for Peace*, in May 1987, asking for an all-Ireland conference.

Adams's political overtures were unknown to the general public, and in 1987 few paid attention to republican political proposals since the IRA campaign dominated the scene. But by the 1980s IRA strategy was not to defeat the British militarily. Instead, the war of attrition they had devised in the late 1970s was in operation, which meant they chose targets for maximum public effect. In the end they believed, as Martin McGuinness said, that they could 'sicken the British' who would then enter talks about withdrawal from Ireland. Huge bombs attracted most publicity. And huge bombs in England captured the attention of the British government in a way those in Ireland did not.

Unfortunately for Adams's peace strategy huge bombs also killed people, often innocent civilians, producing a backlash which made it unthinkable for a British government to engage in dialogue with Sinn Féin. The worst example in this period was the Enniskillen Poppy Day bomb of 8 November 1987, which killed eleven people and injured sixty-three as they gathered to commemorate the dead of two world wars. After a bomb in August 1988 which killed eight soldiers, aged eighteen to twenty-one, and injured nineteen others travelling in a bus to their barracks in Omagh, County Tyrone, Mrs Thatcher introduced a broadcasting ban on Sinn Féin which meant their words could only be heard if dubbed by actors. She also reduced remission for prisoners convicted of terrorist offences.

The British reacted to the new IRA threat by authorising more covert actions by special forces, and the IRA suffered some of its heaviest casualties. In May 1987 the SAS ambushed and killed eight IRA men as they prepared to blow up a police barracks at Loughgall in County Armagh. It was the IRA's greatest loss of life since 1921. In March 1988 the SAS killed three IRA members – Mairéad Farrell, Sean Savage and Danny McCann – in disputed circumstances in Gibraltar. Their funerals, attacked with grenades and gunfire by a fanatic loyalist killer called Michael Stone, led to a chain of deaths amid horrifying scenes in west Belfast when two plain-clothes British soldiers were dragged from their car, beaten, stripped, then shot by the IRA.

With that background it is no wonder that talks between Sinn Féin and the SDLP, which began in January 1988 as a result of Fr Reid's work and continued until September, were strongly criticised by the British government and senior Irish politicians. In fact, it is now known that after the 1986 *árd fheis* republicans had also extended feelers to the British government, feelers not instantly repudiated, though full details of the contacts have yet to be revealed.

INCHING FORWARD

Despite the horrendous violence, the beginning of an IRA campaign against British military targets in Germany and the renewal of an IRA campaign in England in February 1989, the story of the years from 1986 to 1992 on the republican side – in contrast to the negativity from unionism – is one of a developing set of relationships with the British and Irish governments, which became ever more complex and politically risky for the British in view of ongoing IRA attacks, in London in particular.

One crucial figure in this developing relationship was Peter Brooke, who became northern secretary in July 1989. A man with Ulster ancestors, Brooke was knowledgeable about Irish history, well-read, subtle and clever, someone whose bumbling public persona reminded observers of his father, a former British home secretary known as 'Babbling' Brooke. Privately, Brooke was focussed and shrewd. His carefully drafted speeches were designed to encourage Sinn Féin into talks while at the same time not scare off Unionists.

He made two key points in set-piece speeches in 1989 and 1990: first, he admitted that the IRA could not be defeated militarily; and secondly, that Britain had no 'selfish strategic or economic interest' in Ireland. The second point had emerged as a major point of difference in the inconclusive Sinn Féin/SDLP talks in 1988, where John Hume insisted the British were 'neutral' about Ireland but could not allow an IRA campaign to succeed. Gerry Adams retorted that that was like saying the Turks were neutral in Cyprus. Now Brooke was saying, publicly, that Hume was correct. To drive the point home, Brooke even compared the North of Ireland to Cyprus. Unionists were deeply offended.

Even so, Brooke managed to cajole Unionists into talks by engineering a suspension of Anglo-Irish Intergovernmental Council meetings in spring 1991. The talks had come to nothing by July. Nevertheless, they were, incredibly, the first serious talks about a settlement since 1975, although they did not include Sinn Féin, now quite obviously a major player as they had not been in the 1970s. While they did fail, the talks were doubly important: they brought Unionists in from the cold after five years, a major achievement in itself for Brooke; and they were conducted in what became known as a 'three-strand' approach, dealing with relations between the two communities in the North, between north and south, and between Ireland and Britain. It was of considerable significance that Unionists accepted such parameters for talks for it meant they implicitly accepted a role for Dublin in any settlement.

Important as they were, talks in summer 1991 had been unlikely to succeed because a British general election was due before June 1992. The northern parties would not want to give any hostages to fortune in case a snap election was called in autumn 1991. No one was sure what the result of a general election might be because in November 1990, in a major upset in British politics, Margaret Thatcher had resigned as prime minister after eleven years in Downing Street. Her surprise successor as leader of the Conservatives and PM was John Major, a colourless technocratic character with no record of interest in Ireland. Could he win an election in his own right? Few were prepared to bet on him.

8. Peace Process, 1992–1997

The early 1990s was a period of volatility in Irish and British politics. This volatility played an important part in prolonging the process whereby republicans ended their armed campaign against Britain and slowly entered political negotiations. Political uncertainty and divisions in both the London and Dublin governments at various times prevented quick responses to republican overtures and, in the case of John Major, dictated a minimalist approach at all times. It is also true that the agonisingly slow process of decision-making within the republican movement, as Gerry Adams edged cautiously towards recommending an IRA ceasefire, added about a year to the fits and starts which characterised the progress towards peace.

At the opening of the 1990s a political era came to an end as those who had dominated politics in both Ireland and Britain since the 1970s all left the stage within a few years: Garret FitzGerald, Margaret Thatcher, Charles Haughey. In both countries the departure of some of the major figures was not without controversies, which left the parties they had led unsettled for several years thereafter.

In Ireland, Charles Haughey resigned as Taoiseach in January 1992. He was replaced by Albert Reynolds, a shrewd, garrulous, wheeler-dealer, a fixer of a politician, a man backed by those Fianna Fáil TDs who felt that Haughey had excluded them from the spoils of office. Reynolds's denigrators dubbed his supporters in the party the 'country and western tendency', partly because many were from west of the River Shannon, a major geographical and sociological dividing line in Ireland, but also because the largely Dublin-based cabal who had enjoyed Haughey's patronage regarded them as country hicks, or 'culchies' in the parlance of Dublin dwellers. The description was also a none-too-subtle dig at Reynolds himself as he had made money in the 1960s managing dance bands and running ballrooms where country and western music was played. Many within Fianna Fáil regarded Reynolds as a stop-gap leader, not the rightful heir to Charles Haughey.

John Major, the British prime minister, who on the face of it in no way resembled Albert Reynolds, in fact had much in common with him. Major too was a surprise choice as leader in 1990, an outsider, the protégé of Margaret Thatcher. Many in the Conservative party believed she had vastly over-promoted Major into Offices of State rightfully theirs. Like Reynolds, Major inherited many discontented MPs. He too had become prime minister without winning a general election. Some MPs objected to Major because he had failed to support Margaret Thatcher in 1990, others for the simple reason that he was not Margaret Thatcher, an irreplaceable Conservative icon by the time of her departure.

One advantage both men shared was the absence of any of the political or historical baggage about the Irish question which had dogged Haughey and Thatcher. In Haughey's case, the Arms Trial had been an albatross around his neck since 1970. In the case of Margaret Thatcher, her stance during the 1981 hunger strike had earned her undying hatred among republicans. Could the new men succeed where the previous incumbents, for all their charisma, had failed?

Unfortunately, during the years 1991–1997 the legacies of discontent and disgruntlement in the politics of both countries handicapped both men when they faced difficult or controversial issues. Irish governments changed again in 1994 and 1997, coalition partners coming and going, sometimes in bitter acrimony. Reynolds was replaced as Fianna Fáil leader by Bertie Ahern, and as Taoiseach by Fine Gael leader John Bruton. These twists and turns in Dublin had an especially destabilising effect on republicans.

In the early 1990s in Britain the Conservative party began to tear itself apart on the issue of the European Union, a hard-core known as 'Eurosceptics' opposing every move John Major made to bring Britain into line with its EU Treaty obligations. Since the Conservative majority had been reduced to twenty-one after the 1992 general election, Major found it well-nigh impossible to make progress in the face of twenty to thirty committed opponents, some of them Cabinet colleagues. Playing for very high stakes, at times his own political survival, he found it necessary from 1993 on to rely on Ulster Unionist MPs to help push through his policy on Europe, sometimes with a majority of one. Naturally there was a price to pay for the support of Unionists, who had never exhibited any warmth towards the EU. That price was to place a brake on talks with republicans.

This enhanced role for Unionists in the Westminster parliament, coupled with the uncertainties in Dublin, played havoc with what came to be known in 1993 as 'the peace process'. The result was many ups and downs in the years leading to the final IRA ceasefire in 1997. The route was not just bumpy but dotted with signposts to false trails.

The process was well under way by the time of the British general election in April 1992. Many commentators were surprised that John Major won the election, assuming from his unpopularity in opinion polls that the Labour party would win. Politicians in the North of Ireland and Dublin waited anxiously to see how the prime minister, now with his own mandate, would deal with the Irish question.

There was some consternation when he appointed as northern secretary Sir Patrick Mayhew QC MP, a former British attorney-general who had been responsible in the 1980s for some very controversial decisions about security and legal matters in Northern Ireland, including dropping prosecutions against members of the security forces on grounds of 'national security' known only to Mayhew and the intelligence services. Mayhew had given Major his first paid office in politics; it was payback time. Major appointed as Mayhew's number two Michael Mates MP, a former career Army officer who had reached the rank of colonel. Mayhew himself had spent many years in the British Army, rising to become one of its most senior legal officers. Northern nationalists and the Irish government were concerned about what seemed a lurch to the right in the NIO. Unionists were delighted.

SECRET TALKS

Both nationalists and Unionists were wrong. Mayhew continued the secret contacts with the IRA. His security policy towards the IRA was tough, but in August 1992 he banned the UDA, a loyalist organisation which British administrations had scandalously allowed to remain legal despite its being responsible for hundreds of horrific sectarian murders. Mayhew also repeated the assertion that Britain was neutral on Northern Ireland's position within the UK. Albert Reynolds's government breathed a sigh of relief.

A bizarre kind of race then began: bizarre because most of the participants didn't know there was a race. The NIO pressed ahead as fast as they could with so-called all-party talks in the North, which did not include Sinn Féin. Officials hoped to create a coalition of the 'centre' around the UUP and SDLP which would isolate Sinn Féin. Others hoped that if such talks looked likely to succeed republicans might be encouraged to call a ceasefire in order to be included.

On the other hand, Irish officials and senior NIO officials privy to secret talks with the IRA, knew that republicans would not call a ceasefire to enter the existing talks. Before calling a ceasefire the IRA first wanted certain guarantees from the British government as a prelude to an all-embracing settlement. Those guarantees were what they were talking to the British about. Would the talks with northern parties or the talks with the IRA win the race?

Partly to head off any criticism within the republican movement about running down the armed struggle, partly because they believed Mayhew's talks with the political parties were an annoying distraction, and partly because they still believed violence would 'sicken' the British, the IRA stepped up their campaign dramatically in 1992 with a series of colossal bombs in England and the North of Ireland. Belfast was blasted repeatedly and traffic paralysed with hoax bombs. Other town centres across the North were devastated, including Lurgan, County Armagh, by a 1,000lb bomb. In September a 2,000lb bomb wrecked the Forensic Science laboratories in Belfast and also damaged 1,000 homes in a nearby Protestant estate.

But it was an intensified IRA campaign in England which grabbed the headlines on TV and in the press. During 1992 dozens of explosions and hoax bombs had to be dealt with, principally in the greater London area. Often parts of the London Underground were closed, shopping centres evacuated, railway lines blocked, causing massive disruption to commuters and commerce.

In January 1992 a 5lb bomb exploded in Whitehall, London. A bomb was defused at Downing Street in February, but others in London exploded. In March the IRA warned that people in England hadn't 'seen the half of it yet'. In April a giant IRA bomb destroyed the Baltic Exchange in the City of London, killing three people and causing stg£1 billion worth of damage – more than the total cost of all damage caused in the North of Ireland throughout the Troubles, a telling reminder of the North's impoverishment. So it continued to year's end with a 2,000lb bomb defused at London's Canary Wharf in November and a 1,000lb bomb defused in Tottenham Court Road, London, in December, but others exploding in Oxford Street. The hysterical, raging reaction of the British tabloid press to these attacks and their demands for forthright and salutary action against the IRA made any contact between the British government and republicans grounds for political suicide.

Apparently oblivious to the outrage of the British mass media, alongside the bombing Sinn Féin leaders, like Gerry Adams, Martin McGuinness and Mitchell McLaughlin, kept making conciliatory speeches and demanding inclusion in talks, calling their exclusion 'undemocratic'. In the event, Mayhew's multi-party talks collapsed in November 1992. There would be no coalition of the centre to marginalise Sinn Féin. On the contrary, northern politicians began to realise that something was going on behind the scenes to try to bring Sinn Féin into the tent. Sir Patrick

Mayhew made encouraging noises in speeches well telegraphed to the media before delivery, such as one at Coleraine in December 1992 in which he said he detected new thinking in republican circles. Statements by Taoiseach Albert Reynolds and SDLP leader John Hume were beginning to converge with remarks by leading republicans.

What did all this mean? Unionist suspicions grew. The UDA referred to a 'pan-nationalist front', by which they meant a conspiracy among Sinn Féin, SDLP and the Irish government. Unknown to the UDA, they had hit on exactly the combination republicans had been aiming to build since the late 1980s. In February 1993 the UDA, who had been targeting Sinn Féin representatives for some years, began to attack homes of SDLP politicians with blast bombs and blast incendiaries.

HUME–ADAMS

Then, at Easter 1993, effectively confirming UDA suspicions, it was made public that John Hume and Gerry Adams had continued meeting secretly after the public talks between their parties ended in 1988. They issued a joint statement agreeing, in a key phrase, that 'the Irish people as a whole have a right to national self-determination'. Hume immediately came under attack from politicians and commentators in Ireland and Britain, but he insisted he would continue to deal with Adams because he was convinced the IRA wanted to end their campaign.

Maintaining that position was very difficult in the face of ongoing IRA bombs, one of which killed two young boys at Warrington in the northwest of England. In April a massive bomb at Bishopsgate in London killed a journalist and caused hundreds of millions of pounds of damage to the City's financial district. A series of 1,000lb bombs laid waste town centres in Northern Ireland: in Belfast; in the unionist stronghold of Portadown, County Armagh; in Magherafelt, County Derry; in Newtownards, County Down; and in Armagh city. Unionists reacted furiously. The UDA retaliated with random sectarian murders and firebombs at the homes of SDLP politicians. For the first time in the Troubles, loyalists were killing more people than republicans.

Hume pressed on despite growing disquiet in his own party and an appeal from former Taoiseach Garret FitzGerald to break off talks with Adams 'in the very near future'. Finally, in October 1993, Hume submitted to the Irish government the results of his talks with Adams, a paper not for public disclosure which was immediately dubbed 'Hume–Adams'. The two men proposed a joint declaration of principle by the Irish and British governments on Irish self-determination, a declaration that was to be the basis for all-encompassing settlement talks.

Naturally, given its provenance, such a document would have had no chance of success. It would have been anathema to Unionists, nor could either government adopt proposals with Gerry Adams's fingerprints on them. But through their conduits to Hume and the IRA the Irish and British governments had been fully aware of what was going on and were privately drafting their own joint declaration, during the process of which the Irish government had put out feelers to loyalists to encourage them that their aspirations were being catered for. Nevertheless, many Unionists were convinced a political conspiracy against them was afoot.

They had a point. Unionist leaders played no role in the conception or form of the accelerating peace process, and all details of it had been withheld from them: it was a nationalist enterprise, which they believed was driven by their mortal enemies in the IRA. A deep divide emerged in political unionism about how to respond to the apparent change in republicanism. Take it at face value, take it with a large pinch of salt, or reject it entirely?

Many Unionists hoped the process would succeed if it really did lead to peace, but what price would they have to pay? They had no idea, nor were their leaders able to enlighten them. Others were strongly opposed, convinced from the outset that if the process succeeded it could only be at the expense of the unionist community. Concern and apprehension in the Unionist camp manifested itself in an incoherent political response, and in violent reactions from loyalist terrorists and heightened tensions in a society where divisions had been growing wider in every sphere of life.

A PLACE APART

The 1991 census, the first accurate one for thirty years and the first to take full advantage of the detailed enumeration and analysis techniques computers allow, revealed the most segregated society in western Europe. The census showed most people lived in districts which were 90% Catholic, or 90% Protestant. The other districts were heading that way fast.

Division in the North was nothing new. It had always existed in every aspect of society: education, sport, leisure, housing. Nationalists in rural areas tend to play Gaelic football with the same zeal as their compatriots in the rest of the island and with some effect. In consecutive years, 2002 and 2003, Armagh and Tyrone won the All-Ireland football championship in Croke Park,

Dublin. Nationalists support the Republic of Ireland soccer team, always hope England will lose and deride local Northern Ireland football.

Thousands of northern nationalists support Glasgow Celtic. Many travel every weekend to Scotland to watch Celtic play. Equal numbers of unionists support Glasgow Rangers and also travel. The ferry companies prudently provide separate ships for each band of supporters. Polarisation is not restricted to sport with mass followings. Even leisure pursuits which both communities follow, such as golf, have ended up with clubs effectively segregated in many parts of the North because where people live dictates where they relax.

Despite the fact that a movement to promote integrated education has existed since the 1970s, in the 1990s, as today, there was still only a handful of such schools in the North. Ninety-nine percent of Catholic parents opt to send their children to Catholic schools, making the so-called State schools – which in fact have Protestant clergy on their governing bodies – 99% Protestant. Protestant churchmen envy the autonomous Council for Catholic-Maintained Schools; some have asked for a similar body. Ian Paisley has established his own private Free Presbyterian schools. Since the Catholic Church insists on its right to educate the children of Catholic parents, there is no sign there will be any change. The majority of parents, Catholic and Protestant, prefer it the way it is. Besides, given the completely segregated housing conditions in many small towns across the North, in many places there would be virtually no children of the opposite religion to make an integrated school, even if parents wanted one.

The census also confirmed what many had suspected from

the evidence of their eyes, namely that the Catholic population had grown to an all-time high: 42% of the total population. This growth in the Catholic population over the previous thirty years, together with the population shifts caused by the Troubles had produced considerable demographic changes by the 1990s. As a result, in some staunchly unionist towns there were now substantial Catholic enclaves, the most notable being Garvaghy Road in Portadown, the town known as 'the citadel of unionism'.

Another place affected by demographic shifts was Lisburn, declared a city in 2002. Overspill from republican west Belfast resulted in growing numbers of Sinn Féin councillors in the borough and a corresponding rise in loyalist violence directed against Catholic 'incomers'.

The reverse happened in Derry where the dwindling Protestant population moved east across the River Foyle away from the sprawling republican estates of Bogside and Creggan. Some moved further, away from Derry altogether to the Limavady area where, in 2001, they elected the DUP candidate, Gregory Campbell, as MP.

The census figures showed increasing segregation, a growing Catholic population, new Catholic majorities in many towns bringing an end to old political certainties, increasing electoral support for Sinn Féin – all these elements taken together, along with the secretive, nebulous peace process which the British government supported despite ongoing IRA violence, produced an unsettling effect among unionists which continues to the present. Many unionists today wonder where it will all end. The first reaction of many was to say no to change of any kind because it must be for the worse, especially since nationalists were so keen on change.

FORCING THE AGENDA

So it was against that background, in the autumn of 1993, that the secret paperwork flying to and fro between John Hume, Gerry Adams and the Irish and British governments contributed to a serious destabilisation of unionism, from which it has never fully recovered.

In autumn 1993 Northern Ireland went through one of its worst periods of violence, tension and strife. An IRA attempt to kill the UDA leadership went disastrously wrong when a premature bomb detonation killed nine Protestants in a fish shop on the Shankill Road and the IRA bomber himself. In retaliation, the UDA shot dead seven people in a pub at Greysteel, County Derry, as well as six others in different sectarian murders. It seemed the Hume–Adams initiative had been consigned to history when Adams carried the coffin of the Shankill bomber.

In the aftermath of the carnage, John Major tried to placate Unionists by distancing himself from republicans. He foolishly declared to the House of Commons that talking to the IRA would turn his stomach, only for the *Observer* newspaper to reveal that was exactly what Major's government had been doing behind Unionists' backs. The IRA then produced documentation to prove it. Unionists were horrified.

Yet both the Irish and British governments knew from their secret contacts with the IRA that republican leaders did indeed wish to end their campaign. So despite everything, Major and Reynolds and their advisers remained determined to hang on to the opportunity they had. In December 1993 the two leaders published their own Joint Declaration, standing in front of the Downing Street Christmas tree.

The Downing Street Declaration, as it became known, contained much of what republicans had been asking for, though in places the text was deliberately ambivalent. Even so, it was clearly a basis for negotiation. Everything would be on the table. First the IRA would have to call a ceasefire, something many in the movement were adamant they would not do until they got into talks. Ever fearful of a split in the movement, Gerry Adams stalled for time. He asked the Irish government for clarification, then he asked the British government. Would the clarifications be the same? The process dragged on for months.

Another crucial player then stepped onto the stage. President Bill Clinton, elected in November 1992, had committed himself during his election campaign to be proactive on Ireland. He had talked of appointing a 'peace envoy'. During 1993 he had made encouraging noises, but Downing Street did not welcome his intervention. Indeed his relations with John Major's government were distinctly cool. Major and some of his Cabinet colleagues had foolishly interfered in the American election campaign to help President George Bush, even going as far as trawling through British government records to try to dig up dirt on Clinton from his student days at Oxford in the 1960s.

Now, in January 1994, as the British government sought to put Gerry Adams in a box to force him to comply with the Downing Street Declaration, Clinton moved to show Adams how he would be treated if he eschewed violence. Defying furious protests from John Major and against the advice of his own State Department, Clinton gave Adams a three-day visa to visit the USA to address a prestigious foreign affairs conference. During his visit he was given red-carpet treatment, but at the same time was pressurised to accept the Downing Street Declaration and have the IRA call a ceasefire.

It would be another seven months of recriminations between the British government and Sinn Féin before, on 31 August 1994, the IRA announced a 'complete cessation' of military actions. Six weeks later, on 13 October, loyalist terrorist groups, UDA, UVF and Red Hand Commando, calling themselves the Combined Loyalist Military Command, also announced a ceasefire.

Almost immediately a pattern emerged of contrasting responses from the Irish and British governments. Within days of the IRA ceasefire the Taoiseach Albert Reynolds met John Hume and Gerry Adams at Government Buildings, Dublin, and all shook hands at a photo-call. The Irish government announced the establishment of a Forum for Peace and Reconciliation made up of all Irish parties, including Sinn Féin. Unionists boycotted it.

The British government kept Sinn Féin at arm's length. They demanded to know if the ceasefire were permanent and began to talk of handing over weapons, 'decommissioning' they called it, a demand that would become the single biggest obstacle to progress. They refused to meet Sinn Féin until these requirements were satisfied. For more than a year Major's government adopted this slow, begrudging response to the IRA ceasefire, creating hurdles to substantive talks.

Quickly John Major came under pressure from Albert Reynolds and Bill Clinton, who both acted as fast as they could to encourage and reward republicans and show them there were instant benefits for renouncing violence. To no avail. Major was constrained by his tiny majority. Ulster Unionists in the Commons would withdraw their support on crucial European votes if Major made concessions to Sinn Féin: his government would fall.

Major was also assailed by internal party opponents whom he famously dubbed 'the bastards'. Numbered among these were not only Eurosceptic MPs but Cabinet members and senior party figures, like Lord Cranborne, Conservative leader in the House of Lords, who were sympathetic to unionism and sought to frustrate the peace process.

CONFRONTATIONS

Out of the blue, it was the Irish government which fell. Albert Reynolds was forced out as Taoiseach on 17 November 1994 in a controversy surrounding the appointment of the president of the Irish High Court. For the next month there was no effective Irish government as parties jockeyed to form a new coalition. Finally, on 15 December, John Bruton, leader of Fine Gael, was elected Taoiseach at the head of a coalition with Labour and Democratic Left, formerly the Workers' party.

The new Irish government was a source of great anxiety for Sinn Féin. John Bruton had been an opponent of the peace process at the beginning and remained a sceptic. He made no secret of his impatience with the tortuous convolutions of the previous two years, on one occasion snapping at a journalist that he was fed up with 'the fucking peace process'. Bruton had consistently read northern politics wrong, bending over backwards to please Unionists, who simply ignored him. In a famous Freudian slip, on one occasion in the Dáil Albert Reynolds called him 'John Unionist'.

Even more alarming for Sinn Féin was the inclusion in the coalition of Democratic Left led by Proinsias de Rossa, a party which had emerged, after various permutations, from the Official IRA and who were bitter opponents of Sinn Féin north and south, though the days when they had engaged in murderous feuding were long over. The prospect of Proinsias de Rossa in the Cabinet sent a shiver down republicans' spines.

Initially all went well. Bruton bit his lip and went through the motions, picking up the traces where Fianna Fáil's Albert Reynolds had laid them down. In February 1995, in Belfast, he and John Major jointly launched *Frameworks for the Future*, a detailed document worked up by Irish and British officials showing what the nuts and bolts of a settlement might be. Proposing considerable input from Dublin, the document was clearly designed as a come-on to Sinn Féin to entice them into talks. They liked the document. Not surprisingly, the UUP rejected it as a basis for talks. Paisley, as usual, was apoplectic.

But what talks? The British government was still insisting on decommissioning as a pre-condition. As 1995 progressed, Bruton wavered on arms decommissioning, sometimes calling for immediate all-party talks, sometimes appearing to agree with British demands for prior moves on weapons. Powerful strains developed in the republican movement: a year after the ceasefire and still no substantive talks. Was it 1975 all over again? Yes, some cosmetic changes in security by the British, but an actual settlement as far away as ever.

As the first anniversary of the IRA ceasefire loomed at the end of August 1995 republicans were seething. Around this time it looked as though John Bruton might agree decommissioning procedures with the British. He refused to meet John Hume and Gerry Adams together to hear their concerns about the course of events, but Irish government officials were warned of serious tensions in the IRA. It is now known that at this time preparation began of a large bomb for detonation in London.

One of the reasons the British government found it difficult to accede, in summer 1995, to republican demands for talks was the very serious tension developing around the issue of Orange Order marches. In the early 1990s Catholic residents' associations in some flash-point districts had been organising to prevent Orangemen marching through their streets. The fact that the most prominent figures in the residents' associations were republican activists convinced Unionists, suspicious as ever, that the whole campaign was a republican conspiracy. The issue came to a head in Portadown, County Armagh.

Portadown was near where the Orange Order had been founded two hundred years earlier. Orange marches had followed the same route there since the 1820s and Orangemen in the 1990s refused to acknowledge that the fact that the route was no longer a grassy track in the countryside, but a densely populated Catholic district, could or should make any difference. Their demand to march along Garvaghy Road regardless became symbolic of wider unionist resistance to any change in northern society and refusal to acknowledge the new demography. They were supported through the late 1990s by unionists opposing the peace process and later the Good Friday Agreement.

The result every year until 2001 was a ritual violent stand-off at the picturesque and once-remote Church of Ireland church at Drumcree, at the country end of the Garvaghy Road. The stand-off involved hundreds of British troops and police, but was also associated with widespread loyalist disturbances and intimidation of Catholics across the North. In scenes which looked like a movie of a medieval battle and which provided wonderful television pictures but terrible publicity for unionists, thousands of be-sashed Orangemen waving brightly coloured flags and banners milled around on the slope below the spire of Drumcree church. Each year hundreds of soldiers and 1,000 police in full riot gear positioned themselves behind coils of razor wire and defended a moat dug by earth-movers by firing plastic bullets into the Orange mobs. Each year until 1998 the police finally gave in to Orange intimidation and forced a route for them, batoning Catholic residents who would stage a sit-in on the Garvaghy Road. Other residents would then attack the police with anything they could lay their hands on. The scenes caused deep disgust and alienation to the North's Catholics; it was the point of no return in the deteriorating relationship between the Catholic community and the RUC.

The first serious confrontation occurred in 1995 when Ian Paisley, in a typically incendiary speech, pronounced the march to be of fundamental importance, a symbol of the birthright of Ulstermen. It was do or die. The seventy-five-year-old Molyneaux, the UUP leader, was silent and invisible during the clashes at Portadown that summer whereas, as well as Paisley, David Trimble, the district's MP, played a leading and very publicly aggressive role in support of the Orange Order's demands.

Drumcree 1995, coming after the *Frameworks* document of February that year, seems to have been the final nail in the political coffin of party leader Jim Molyneaux. Frustrated party stalwarts asked why he had been unable to stop the British government developing policy links with Dublin despite having a parliamentary armlock on John Major. At the Ulster Unionist Council meeting in March, Molyneaux was re-elected leader, but a 'stalking-horse' candidate who stood against him had received 15% of the vote. After the riot-torn summer, Molyneaux resigned on 28 August.

On 8 September, David Trimble was elected UUP leader, largely, it appeared, on the strength of his uncompromising attitude at Portadown. He was regarded as the most hardline of the leadership candidates. Trimble lost no time in setting out his stall, demanding elections to a powerless northern convention of all parties. Its role would be to initiate talks in some manner he did not specify.

Still there was no resolution in sight to the question of IRA weapons and no all-party talks. President Clinton visited Belfast in November, the first serving US president to do so. He was received rapturously at a rally in front of City Hall. He shook hands with Gerry Adams in front of the world's media and endorsed former US Senate majority leader George Mitchell, who had been deputed to head an international body to try to resolve the decommissioning issue.

When Mitchell did report, on 24 January 1996, he recommended that decommissioning and talks should proceed in tandem. He also produced what came to be known as the 'Mitchell Principles', a set of non-violent democratic criteria for entering talks. John Major said he accepted the report but in fact ignored it, insisting paramilitaries should begin decommissioning before talks. He also announced an election in the North to a powerless 'Forum' where all parties would engage in debate about peace talks. It seemed exactly what David Trimble had asked for. Nationalists were outraged. For the IRA's leaders it was the last straw. It meant further months of delay. Even John Bruton said an election was pouring petrol on a fire.

On 9 February 1996 a 1,000lb IRA bomb exploded at Canary Wharf, in London's Docklands, killing two men and causing immense damage. Almost simultaneously came a statement from the IRA announcing the end of its seventeen-month ceasefire. The bomb galvanised John Major and John Bruton who, on 28 February, set 10 June 1996 as the date for all-party talks, although Sinn Féin would be excluded until there was a new IRA ceasefire. The peace process was in complete disarray.

It was clear John Major could not deliver. His party was in open revolt, his government sagging towards the end of its term. There had to be a British general election by May 1997, so no northern party leader would stick his neck out in the months before such a poll. The preparatory talks which began in summer 1996, chaired by Senator Mitchell, did agree on procedures for talks but quickly broke up amid mutual recriminations. When they resumed in the autumn, after the worst summer of sectarian violence for a decade, the atmosphere was even more bitter. Everyone marked time until the British general election.

9. *Agreement and Disagreement,*
1997–2007

Four years of dithering, frustration and impotence, which marred the contribution of John Major's government to the Irish peace process, ended on 1 May 1997 when Tony Blair's New Labour party won the British general election with a landslide. Blair's majority of 179 in a parliament of 659 was unprecedented in modern times. Political pundits had to look back ninety years to the 1906 Liberal victory to find a comparable rout of the Conservatives. The following month, after a general election in the Republic, Bertie Ahern was elected Taoiseach to head what would be a stable, Fianna Fáil-led coalition. The uncertainties which had dogged the politics of the early 1990s were over. The scene was set for rapid progress.

Here at last was an opportunity to test the basic hypothesis Irish and British governments had subscribed to for decades, namely that in the absence of an armed campaign by republicans the two communities in the North could agree structures for running the State.

Blair's government hit the ground running. In contrast to the fits and starts of the previous four years, in the period 1997–2001 the North of Ireland saw more change than in the previous generation. By the strictest definition the 'Troubles' came to an end in 1997 with a renewed IRA ceasefire and the end of major organised loyalist terrorism against Catholics. Nevertheless, the very speed and radical nature of change produced stress fractures in both republican and loyalist organisations, which ensured that low-level violence continued.

Loyalist violence, by the 1990s more common and regular than republican violence, tended to be marked by bursts of murderous feuding among factions in the greater Belfast area as the largest loyalist terrorist group, the UDA, disintegrated into local criminal baronies competing in the drug trade. By 2000 there was no political objective directing loyalist violence. The hundreds of crude pipe bombs the UDA threw at the homes of Catholics in Belfast and County Antrim towns were simple naked intimidation to force Catholics out of certain districts.

Republican violence was now dominated by two groups splintered from the mainstream IRA – the Continuity IRA (CIRA) and the Real IRA (RIRA). These groups continued bombing after 1997 in an unpredictable and desultory fashion, but no less deadly for that. Indeed a baleful combination of RIRA and CIRA members was responsible for the biggest casualty toll from a single bomb in the Troubles. At Omagh, on 15 August 1998, twenty-eight civilians and two unborn twins were killed by a 500lb bomb that destroyed the central shopping area of the town.

The IRA, although on ceasefire – which they interpreted as an end to attacks on British soldiers and police and loyalist terrorists – continued to carry out punishment shootings in the districts where they exercised control, to kill drug-dealers and to wage an undeclared campaign against members of RIRA, killing and maiming them.

Nonetheless, for the first time in a generation politics dominated events in the North. Tony Blair's gigantic majority gave him irresistible power. Unionists who had forced John Major to prevaricate since the first IRA ceasefire in 1994, in return for supporting EU policy decisions that were controversial in domestic British politics, now found themselves without any parliamentary leverage. Furthermore, aside from the fact that the British Labour party was traditionally lukewarm towards unionism, Unionists knew they could expect no favours after their parliamentary tactics supporting John Major in the previous four years. It was also clear that, because of the British 'first past the post' electoral system, even if Blair lost one hundred seats at the next election he would still remain prime minister.

Unionists got off to a very poor start with the new government by their extraordinarily bad treatment of Mo Mowlam, the feisty new Labour secretary of state. There had never been a female northern secretary before, but in any case the very conservative, prim, correct Unionist politicians reacted badly to Mowlam, first as a woman politician, secondly because she was famously fluent with four-letter words. Rev. Ian Paisley was flabbergasted. Unionists also strenuously objected to her chummy *bonhomie* with Sinn Féin members whom they insisted should be kept at arm's length. In the end, David Trimble ignored Mowlam and dealt with Blair.

Blair made it clear at the outset that he wanted all-party talks as soon as possible and that all-party talks meant talks including Sinn Féin. On 16 May 1997 he authorised contacts between his officials and Sinn Féin. It was made known to republicans that in the event of an IRA ceasefire there would be a complete transformation in the attitude of the British government, and that Sinn Féin would be admitted to talks within weeks.

Blair refused to be deflected by the shocking murders of

two RUC men shot in the back in Lurgan on 16 June. He and Ahern presented joint proposals on decommissioning along the lines of Senator Mitchell's January 1996 report. An international commission would be established to supervise the process of decommissioning republican and loyalist weapons. It would be chaired by a Canadian general, John de Chastelain, acceptable because he had no connections with Ireland, north or south. Blair then set 15 September as the date for all-party talks, with a deadline of May 1998 for agreement.

Many thought it was all impossibly optimistic, yet despite negative predictions and an upsurge in loyalist violence instigated yet again by the Orange Order's demand to assert their traditional right to march along the Catholic Garvaghy Road, republicans believed Blair. So the IRA announced a 'complete cessation of military operations from midday, 20 July'.

Gerry Adams, John Hume and Bertie Ahern met in Dublin on 25 July and, quoting a key phrase from Senator Mitchell's principles governing talks, issued a statement expressing commitment to 'exclusively democratic and peaceful methods'. The peace process was on track again.

Unionists had deep misgivings. They were being hustled into talks under conditions they had said they would never accept, chief among them being the existence of the IRA's intact arsenal. Although both governments paid lip service, in 1997 no one except Unionists took that issue seriously. Michael Oatley, the MI6 go-between who had met the IRA over many years until 1993, said that harping on about decommissioning was 'an excuse to avoid the pursuit of peace'. Unionists were also convinced that the Irish and British governments regarded them as the problem and were conniving with Sinn Féin to cobble a deal together as fast as possible, oblivious to unionist susceptibilities.

As the time for convening all-party talks approached, the British government worked hard to disabuse Unionists of these suspicions, but failed. In contrast to the united front that Ahern, Hume and Adams presented, the divisions within unionism about whether or not to talk to Sinn Féin, which had existed since the start of the peace process, developed into serious fissures, which are even wider today. Ian Paisley led his party out of the process in protest at Sinn Féin's inclusion. Only after a lengthy meeting in September 1997 did the UUP executive consent to David Trimble going into talks. Many senior UUP figures remained unconvinced. The IRA ceasefire was less than two months old. The simmering animosities from another summer's Drumcree-provoked violence had barely cooled.

THREE-STRAND APPROACH

Nevertheless, on 15 September Trimble and his UUP team entered Stormont flanked by representatives of loyalist micro-parties the PUP and the UDP, political fronts for the terrorist groups the UVF and UDA respectively. It was a gesture of solidarity which earned nationalist contempt, but without these parties, tenuous as their support for the process might be, Trimble and his UUP team would have cut lonely figures.

It is now known that the apparently united front on the nationalist side masked dangerous splits in the republican movement about the parameters of talks and the Mitchell Principles, to which Sinn Féin had to subscribe in order to enter talks. The logic of these principles meant the eventual disappearance of the IRA. Yet loyalist violence continued. Matters came to a head at an IRA meeting in Gweedore, County Donegal, in October when a section of the IRA, led by former quartermaster-general Michael McKevitt, broke away and set up the so-called Real IRA.

The talks format, agreed in 1996 while Sinn Féin was still in purdah, operated in three strands: internal northern affairs; north-south relations; and east-west relations between Dublin and London. The talks were driven by officials from Blair's Cabinet Office, the NIO, the Taoiseach's Office and the Department of Foreign Affairs in Dublin, many of whom knew each other from years of negotiations. Strand Three was easiest: there was little at odds between the two governments.

The overall formula, which became something of a mantra, was that 'nothing is agreed until everything is agreed'. This formula meant that both sets of government officials could present proposals which, even if some parties rejected them, could still remain the basis for proposals on the same issues, but would not prevent any parties revisiting the issues again and unpicking the proposals. It was tedious and mind-numbing.

Sinn Féin was anxious to maximise Strand Two, north-south relations, and to minimise Strand One, internal northern affairs. While the SDLP shared that emphasis to some extent, their priority was to get a partnership arrangement established for the North in Strand One. The UUP also concentrated on Strand One. Their aim was to diminish Strand Two as much as possible. By Christmas virtually no progress had been made. Sinn Féin wouldn't even talk about an assembly in the North. These conflicting objectives led one participant to dub the procedure 'the riddle of the strands', a play on the title of the famous 1903 spy novel by the republican activist Erskine Childers.

Relations between the parties were often poisonous. At no stage in the whole process did Unionists speak to any Sinn Féin delegate. Indeed David Trimble did not shake Gerry Adams's hand until July 2003. Even so, despite the lack of progress when the talks broke up for Christmas 1997, five UUP MPs were sufficiently concerned about the direction of the talks to issue a warning statement. They included the youngest Unionist MP, thirty-four-year-old Jeffrey Donaldson, who had been the agent, then successor in the Lagan Valley seat of the former UUP leader Lord Molyneaux. Donaldson had had a number of relatives killed by the IRA in the Troubles. Clearly the five MPs would have been happy to end the talks then.

In the New Year the process entered a very rocky patch indeed. On 27 December Billy Wright, a notorious loyalist killer and leader of a breakaway UVF faction, the Loyalist Volunteer Force (LVF), was shot dead in jail by INLA prisoners. In January 1998 his LVF faction carried out a series of sectarian murders in retaliation, aided by elements in the UDA in Belfast. More murders followed involving the INLA and IRA, who shot a drug-dealer and a prominent UDA man.

In January, as a result of the murders, the UDA's front party, the UDP, was suspended from the talks, then in February Sinn Féin was expelled for two weeks. At one stage, in January, when it had looked as though the loyalist ceasefire would break down, the secretary of state Mo Mowlam went to the Maze prison to persuade prisoners to support the process. Tony Blair said she had 'saved the day'.

GOOD FRIDAY AGREEMENT

Into this unpromising atmosphere the two governments had introduced, in January, a short document called 'Heads of Agreement', indicating an overall plan which they said was their 'best guess at what might be generally acceptable'. The plan included a northern assembly, cross-border bodies and an east-west structure. Nationalists were apprehensive that human rights and equality seemed to have been set at a discount. Sinn Féin formally rejected it, as did the IRA, saying it was a surrender to Unionist demands. Nevertheless, in what Dublin and London regarded as a breakthrough, the parties agreed to discuss the document. The governments' view proved correct: in the end the final Agreement was not too far away from the skeleton plan sketched out in January.

In retrospect it can be seen that the two months from January were spent with the parties circling each other and preparing supporters for an outcome far short of the demands each party had made on entry to the talks. The chairman, Senator Mitchell, convinced the elements of an agreement were present, set a deadline of 9 April for the talks.

Tony Blair and Bertie Ahern arrived in Belfast for the final days and President Clinton worked the telephone from Washington night and day, keeping pressure on the party leaders. Both Trimble's UUP and Gerry Adams's Sinn Féin went to the deadline and beyond, seventeen hours beyond in fact, so that the Agreement was not endorsed until 5.00pm on 10 April, Good Friday. The reasons for that last-minute delay have dogged the Agreement's operation ever since.

The priority had been to establish structures of administration: an assembly to run northern departments, like education, environment, health and so on; a north-south ministerial council; all-Ireland implementation bodies for matters such as tourism, fisheries and language; a new British–Irish Intergovernmental Council; and a British–Irish Council bringing together representatives from the devolved UK regions and the two sovereign governments. Many other critical matters could not be agreed, however, and were left to a series of commissions to resolve. Herein has lain the source of continuing disagreement which has brought the administrative structures crashing down repeatedly since 1998. The Agreement was essentially negotiated between Trimble's Ulster Unionists and Hume's SDLP, the two governments still following the aim of creating a coalition of the centre. The UUP, however, remained fixated on Sinn Féin and the IRA, in fact always referring to the party as 'Sinn Féin/IRA'.

The major areas of disagreement were all between the UUP and Sinn Féin, with whom the UUP refused to negotiate: policing, criminal justice, demilitarisation and, of course, weapons decommissioning, the original objection Unionists had raised in 1994. All these issues remain to be resolved today despite repeated meetings since 1998 involving Tony Blair, Bertie Ahern and the northern parties to the Agreement.

The unpalatable truth is that if the parties could not agree on these issues in talks, then the recommendations of any commission would not find universal acceptance among the same parties. Policing was the touchstone for Sinn Féin. Chris Patten, former Conservative party chairman, who was appointed to chair the commission on policing, was never going to recommend the disbandment of the RUC, which Sinn Féin demanded as their bottom line. Apart from the obvious question of what would happen in the interim if the force were disbanded, Unionists would never have accepted such a proposal. As it was, Patten's radical report transforming policing in the North caused convulsions among Unionists which have not yet subsided.

Patten changed the name of the police from RUC to the Police Service of Northern Ireland (PSNI), and decreed police stations should be neutral workplaces and therefore the Union Jack flag must not fly nor pictures of Queen Elizabeth be displayed. The uniform was also redesigned, softened from the sharp, militaristic RUC tunic and cap to a variety of options, including baseball caps, jerkins, open-neck shirts. The most controversial measure was that, in order to remedy the huge religious imbalance of the force being 93% Protestant in a society which is now only 57% Protestant, recruitment should be on a 50/50 Catholic/Protestant basis. These were the most fundamental changes to the ethos and organisation of the North's police force since the establishment of that force in 1921.

Radical as they were, the changes were not enough to satisfy Sinn Féin, which still holds out for the abolition of Special Branch, the intelligence-gathering wing of the police, and greater control by the Policing Board which oversees the PSNI. Sinn Féin refuses to take up its seats on the Board, or to encourage young nationalists to join the police until its demands are met.

UNIONISM DIVIDED

The major tussle has been between Sinn Féin and David Trimble's UUP on weapons decommissioning: the Unionist touchstone. That issue almost prevented agreement emerging in April 1998.

Because of creative ambiguity in the wording of the Agreement, Trimble insisted on a letter from Tony Blair to guarantee him that Sinn Féin would be excluded from office if the IRA did not decommission. Of course the letter was worthless since it was not incorporated in the Agreement itself. Knowing the UUP had lost on that point, Jeffrey Donaldson MP left Stormont on Good Friday before the Agreement was signed and fought an increasingly bitter battle within the UUP to prevent David Trimble working the machinery of the Agreement until the IRA has decommissioned its weapons.

Donaldson's criticisms struck a chord among the wider unionist community in 1998 and support for his position has grown ever since. Ian Paisley's DUP took no part in the negotiations and opposed the Good Friday Agreement from the word go, DUP deputy leader Peter Robinson MP describing it as 'a turbo-charged model of Sunningdale, the Anglo-Irish Agreement with a vengeance, a fully armed version of the Framework Document'. Hardly.

Their opposition convinced many unionists. In the referendum to endorse the Good Friday Agreement, held in May 1998, an exit poll showed only 55% of unionists supported it compared to 96% of nationalists. Some would put the true unionist figure at 51%. It was only due to the overwhelming nationalist support that the overall figure in the referendum was 71% in favour, but the distance between the two communities widened in the years following the referendum so that by 2002 most polls showed a majority of unionists opposed to the Agreement and indicating they would vote against it in any new referendum.

In the 1998 election to the assembly established by the

Agreement, Trimble's UUP just managed to secure a majority of unionist votes against vociferous opposition from Paisley's DUP and a number of unionist splinter groups. With the SDLP, which secured a majority of the nationalist vote, Trimble could set up a power-sharing administration. The main snag for Trimble was that the executive of that administration had to include the main parties in proportion to their numbers in the assembly, and that meant including Sinn Féin. Ian Paisley's party simply refused to sit alongside Sinn Féin ministers in an executive. Many in the unionist community agreed with their position.

The division within the unionist community was mirrored in the UUP where the party leader, David Trimble, repeatedly faced challenges led by Jeffrey Donaldson, but each time managed to gain the support of only 55% of his party's ruling council to continue operating the Agreement's institutions. Each time Trimble has returned to operate the institutions after a collapse, his involvement has been conditional and lukewarm, with pre-conditions and ultimatums. Finally, Donaldson resigned from the UUP and in January 2004 joined the DUP, along with his former UUP colleagues, assembly members Arlene Foster and Noreen Beare.

Even before Donaldson's departure, defections from his party meant that by 2001 Trimble could no longer command a majority of Unionist votes in the assembly. His position within unionism was fatally weakened by repeated allegations about IRA activity, culminating in arrests of Sinn Féin officials in October 2002 and the levelling against them of charges of espionage in government offices at Stormont. The assembly and executive instantly collapsed. The political process went into suspended animation. Sinn Féin and Unionists exchanged increasingly heated recriminations.

In an attempt to lance the boil, Bertie Ahern and Tony Blair issued a Joint Declaration in Hillsborough at Easter 2003, containing a timetable for implementing those parts of the Agreement not yet in operation and requiring 'acts of completion' from both republicans and Unionists. They required that the IRA must cease all paramilitary activity and that in return Unionists must agree to work the machinery of the Agreement. The two premiers demanded an unequivocal statement from Gerry Adams indicating there would be no more IRA activity. When the statement Adams made in April 2003 proved unsatisfactory to the Irish and British governments because Adams declined to say IRA activity 'would' end, Tony Blair postponed the assembly elections due in May 2003.

It was clear to both governments from their own private polling in spring 2003 that unionist mistrust had grown so much that in any elections David Trimble's UUP would lose out to Ian Paisley's DUP, who were pledged not to work the Agreement. It was equally clear that nationalist frustration with Unionist foot-dragging would mean Sinn Féin would overtake the SDLP as they had already done in the 2001 British general election, winning four MPs to the SDLP's three.

As a consequence, Martin McGuinness, former IRA chief-of-staff, would be eligible to be Deputy First Minister of the North's administration, an outcome no Unionist, least of all anyone in the DUP, would contemplate. The Agreement's northern institutions, predicated as they were on a deal between UUP and SDLP, simply would not function.

Six months of negotiations between Sinn Féin and the UUP

almost reached fruition in October 2003 when, in return for a previously agreed statement from Gerry Adams and another slice of decommissioning from the IRA, Tony Blair announced an assembly election on 26 November. As the carefully arranged sequence of events unfolded on 21 October, David Trimble stepped before the cameras and announced, to the consternation of all concerned, that he was putting the process 'on hold' because the IRA decommissioning was not 'transparent'. It had been carried out in secret at an unknown location, though to the satisfaction of General John de Chastelain, the man appointed to supervise the process.

A month later Trimble led his deeply divided party into elections, with several of his candidates sounding like DUP candidates. His opponents inside and outside the party castigated him for being a naïve and inept negotiator who had made a deal with Sinn Féin without tying down the part of the deal which was most important to him. Within the unionist community he lost the election to Ian Paisley's DUP who were united in their opposition to the Good Friday Agreement.

As expected in the nationalist community, Sinn Féin comprehensively defeated the SDLP with a swing of 5%. It seems that both communities elected their toughest negotiators to go into the review of the operation of the Agreement scheduled for February 2004.

THE END OF THE TROUBLES?

Many observers believed that the DUP's victory over the UUP was necessary in order to have a fully inclusive political process, that while the DUP remained outside the tent the UUP could not give its whole-hearted support to the Agreement for fear of being outflanked by their hardline rivals.

Now, forty years after the Divis Street riots in 1964, Paisley had finally taken over as leader of unionism, an outcome few foresaw and both Dublin and London dreaded. Fewer still believed he would ever negotiate with Sinn Féin, much less work an administration in the North with them. What would the DUP do with the new responsibility they had acquired as the dominant political force in unionism?

The DUP had resolutely opposed the Good Friday Agreement and the consequent referendums in both parts of Ireland. Their election win raised serious questions: could Sinn Féin and the DUP ever agree on structures to run the North? Would Ian Paisley and his DUP agree to pay the price for devolved administration in the North, namely to share power with Sinn Féin and participate in all-Ireland bodies?

At first it seemed the answer to these questions was no. In March 2004, the planned review of the Good Friday Agreement broke up, the DUP refusing even to speak to Sinn Féin. Ian Paisley insisted on full decommissioning and the disbandment of the IRA before any negotiations; on the face of it, impossible demands. Gerry Adams's position was that there would be full decommissioning and the IRA would stand down only after a satisfactory settlement. Again and again those two issues prevented any progress towards establishing political institutions.

Nevertheless, despite the deadlock, in a real sense the troubles were over. Sectarian killings had ceased. No one believed the IRA would resume its armed struggle. No one in the nationalist community wanted them to. This real change in the North meant that the election result in November 2003 caused a political crisis, not a terrorist crisis. The British government announced plans to withdraw thousands of troops by 2005.

The priority of the two governments was now to re-establish political institutions. At various times in the next two years they whisked the Northern parties to grandiose locations to try to hammer out a deal in hothouse talks. On each occasion the same obstacles surfaced: the DUP would not talk to Sinn Féin before its demands on weapons and the IRA were met, and Sinn Féin would not budge without guarantees that the DUP would operate the Good Friday Agreement's institutions.

In September 2004 after intensive talks in Leeds Castle in Kent it appeared there had been some movement. Officials from the British and Irish governments had drafted a blueprint for the parties to sign up to, but the DUP was insisting on photographic proof of IRA decommissioning. In return republicans that indicated that they would allow two clergymen to observe decommissioning. The governments pressed ahead and pinned their hopes on a 'comprehensive agreement' between Sinn Féin and the DUP before Christmas. That prospect foundered when Paisley, in what Adams called an 'offensive' speech, demanded republicans wear 'sackcloth and ashes' to show repentance for their campaign of violence.

Any slim hope of progress were dashed on 20 December 2004 when the head office of the Northern Bank in Belfast was robbed in a brilliantly executed operation. The robbers drove off with truckloads of banknotes amounting to the sum of £26.5 million (€37 million). No one knows the full total of foreign currency stolen. Despite furious denials from Sinn Féin, all the evidence pointed to the IRA. The bank heist enraged both the Irish and British governments. They regarded it as a betrayal and proof that the IRA remained fully operational and engaged in criminal enterprises.

Republicans' difficulties were compounded in January 2005 when IRA members were implicated in a brutal murder outside a bar in central Belfast. Sinn Féin's normally faultless media performance faltered under a media campaign by the victim's sisters and condemnation from Irish, British and American politicians including Senator Edward Kennedy who said it was time for the IRA to disband. The British government said no further talks were possible until the IRA 'resolved its position'.

To make matters worse, a British general election was looming in May. Would Sinn Féin suffer? In a gesture obviously made with the election in mind, Gerry Adams publicly asked the IRA to 'fully embrace and accept democratic means'. The implication was that if Sinn Féin did well in the general election the IRA would then be vindicated in standing down.

In the event, both Sinn Féin and the DUP prospered in the election. Sinn Féin raised their Westminster total to five seats over the SDLP's three, but the DUP's performance was spectacular. They took nine seats including that of the UUP leader David Trimble and reduced the UUP to one seat: a sweet victory for Ian Paisley.

This election result confirmed the domination of the DUP and Sinn Féin: the 2003 assembly elections had not been a blip. Immediately both British and Irish governments acted on the new realities and set out to woo the DUP – now the unchallenged leaders of unionism by a mile. Promises were made to individual

MPs. Money was earmarked for unionist districts. Controversial appointments favoured by the DUP were made to public bodies.

On the republican side the summer of 2005 also saw momentous developments. Sinn Féin accepted they would have to deal with the DUP, but to do so republicans would have to move. On 28 July the IRA made a public statement declaring its war over, and ordering volunteers to dump arms. On 26 September General de Chastelain declared that all IRA weapons had been decommissioned, witnessed by two clergymen.

Powerful political pressure now bore down on the DUP. With all their demands met how could they refuse to deal with republicans? On 6 April 2006 Prime Minister, Tony Blair, and Taoiseach, Bertie Ahern, came to Belfast and presented a road map towards devolution. The assembly would be recalled on 15 May and a deadline of 24 November set for establishing an executive. If the parties failed to do so all the institutions would be closed down and a new 'Plan B' put in place. In effect the two governments would run the North in what would be joint authority.

By October, when no progress at all had been made, the two governments brought the parties to St Andrews in Scotland for a last ditch effort before the 24 November deadline. Both Blair and Ahern were personally anxious for success. Blair had announced he would leave office in summer 2007 and Ahern had his third general election in the Republic also scheduled for summer 2007. They had each devoted a decade to the Northern process.

They announced the governments-sponsored 'St Andrews Agreement'. A 'transitional assembly' would meet from 24 November. If it appeared that an executive was possible then an assembly election would be called early in 2007, but if no agreement was reached after that election then Stormont would be shut down and Plan B installed.

The DUP had one final requirement, one the two governments shared: Sinn Féin must support the police in the North. They could hardly share in running an administration otherwise. It was a huge hurdle for republicans, but Gerry Adams had prepared the ground well. After a series of huge meetings in republican strongholds like west Belfast and mid-Ulster a special *Ard Fheis* of 900 delegates was called on 28 January 2007. They voted overwhelmingly to support the PSNI. On 30 January Blair called an assembly election for 7 March.

Once again the DUP and Sinn Féin triumphed over their rivals qualifying Ian Paisley and Martin McGuinness to be First and Deputy First Ministers in an executive. Would it, could it happen? As the deadline of 26 March approached the DUP were demanding more time. There was disquiet among their supporters about even contemplating sharing power with Sinn Féin.

Then on the day itself, to the frank amazement of observers, television news beamed pictures of the unthinkable: Gerry Adams and Ian Paisley sitting side by side. They announced a power-sharing executive would be established on 8 May.

And so it was. In the presence of Tony Blair and Bertie Ahern, the two peace-brokers, DUP and Sinn Féin ministers took office. 'A new era', Adams called it. After his re-election as Taoiseach on 14 June, Bertie Ahern said 8 May was not, as many thought, the end of history in the North, but only the beginning.

Appendices
I. Glossary of Terms

Apprentice Boys of Derry One of the Protestant 'Loyal Orders', it organises annual demonstrations commemorating the events surrounding the Siege of Derry in 1688 when apprentices closed the city's gates on the approach of the army of King James II. With about 10,000 members, the Order's major demonstration in Derry each August has often been the occasion of increased tension and violence.

Ard Fheis The name Irish political parties give to their annual conference.

Armalite An American rifle favoured by the IRA.

Army Council The seven-member ruling body of the IRA which determines its military strategy.

Articles 2 & 3 Articles in the 1937 Irish Constitution (Bunreacht na hÉireann) defining the 'national territory' as the island of Ireland and regarded as laying claim to the six northern counties which constitute Northern Ireland (*see* Six Counties).

B Specials Established in 1920 to defend Northern Ireland against the IRA. An exclusively Protestant, part-time force abolished in 1969 and replaced by the Ulster Defence Regiment (UDR) in 1970.

Belfast confetti Rivets and pieces of small, dense, heavy ironmongery thrown with terrible effect by shipyard workers in Belfast riots.

Dáil The lower house of the Irish parliament.

E4A The RUC's covert surveillance unit, part of 'E' division, or Special Branch.

Garda Síochána (Keepers of Peace) Normally known as the Gardaí, the police force of the Irish Republic.

Gerrymandering The deliberate redrawing of electoral boundaries to control the outcome of elections. The term originates from 1812 when the governor of Massachusetts, Elbridge Gerry, drew the boundaries for a congressional district that looked like a salamander. His opponents called it a 'Gerrymander'.

H-blocks Compounds in the Maze prison, so named because of their shape. Each had approximately two hundred cells in four wings.

Irish National Liberation Army (INLA) An extreme republican paramilitary group established in 1974.

Long Kesh The name of a Second World War airfield, located sixteen kilometres south of Belfast, whose wartime Nissen huts were used to house republican internees in 1971. The name was later changed to HM Prison Maze when permanent facilities were built. Republicans never used the new name.

Loyalist Volunteer Force (LVF) A dissident faction of the UVF formed in the late 1990s.

Northern Ireland Civil Rights Association (NICRA) Established in 1967 and modelled on the American black civil rights movement's tactics of passive resistance and non-violence.

Northern Ireland Office (NIO) The department of the British government established in 1972 to administer Northern Ireland under direct rule from Westminster through a secretary of state who has a seat in the British Cabinet.

Orange Order The largest of the 'Loyal Orders', it was founded in County Armagh in 1795 and expanded into an important politico-religious grouping opposed to Irish nationalism. Throughout its existence its traditions of marching, sometimes through nationalist districts, has caused controversy. Its extensive programme of marches culminates on 12 July to commemorate the victory of King William III at the Battle of the Boyne in 1690.

Peaceline Originally high fences made from corrugated metal, these were erected by the British Army in 1969 to provide a physical barrier between Catholic and Protestant districts. Most are now permanent brick, or concrete structures.

Plastic bullet Officially described as a plastic baton round (PBR), it is a controversial riot-control weapon used extensively from February 1973. A solid PVC cylinder, when fired its muzzle velocity is estimated to be in excess of 250kph. In 1998 a parliamentary answer revealed that plastic and rubber bullets killed sixteen persons since 1970. A total of 124,829 plastic and rubber bullets (*see* Rubber bullets) were fired between 1970 and November 1998.

Proportional representation A voting system designed to give seats to parties in proportion to the number of votes cast for each party rather than, as in the USA and Britain, the system of first past the post, or 'winner takes all'. Proportional representation ensures seats for minority parties and is widely used throughout Europe.

Provisional Irish Republican Army (PIRA) Generally simply known as the IRA, it is the largest republican paramilitary group. Following a split from the Official IRA in 1969, its violent campaign proceeded for almost three decades.

PSNI Police Service of Northern Ireland. The title of the new police service inaugurated in the North of Ireland on 4 November 2001 on the recommendation of the Patten report.

Rolling devolution A scheme devised by British secretary of state Jim Prior in 1982 by which devolved powers would be 'rolled out' to local parties the more they cooperated with each other in sharing power. Nationalists boycotted the scheme.

Royal Ulster Constabulary (RUC) The police force for Northern Ireland, established in 1921.

Rubber bullet A riot-control weapon, it was replaced by plastic bullets in 1975. According to official figures, 55,688 rubber bullets were fired between 1970 and 1975.

'Shoot-to-kill' policy A description coined by the SDLP security spokesman Michael Canavan to describe incidents when security forces in the North shot dead suspected republicans at road checks in disputed circumstances.

Six Counties The name by which nationalists, but especially republicans, refer to Northern Ireland, which is comprised of the six counties of Antrim, Down, Armagh, Tyrone, Fermanagh and Derry, which unionists call Londonderry.

Special Air Service (SAS) A special forces unit of the British Army officially known as 22 SAS Regiment, it was formally deployed in Northern Ireland in 1976 and has been involved in several disputed killings.

Stormont The building, completed in 1929, which housed the Northern Ireland parliament until it was prorogued in 1972. It became the seat of the assembly established after the 1998 Good Friday Agreement. The term 'Stormont' is also used to refer to the Unionist government of the period 1921–1972.

Taoiseach Literally meaning 'chief', it is the term for the Irish prime minister.

TD A member of the Dáil, the Irish parliament (in full, *Teachta Dála*).

'The Falls' An abbreviation for the Falls Road, but its meaning widened over the twentieth century to include the many streets of the republican heartland of west Belfast, close to the city centre.

'The Shankill' An abbreviation for the Shankill Road, but, like the Falls Road a few hundred metres away, a term which includes the streets of the loyalist heartland of west Belfast.

Ulster Defence Association (UDA) The largest loyalist paramilitary organisation, the UDA was established in Belfast in 1971 and finally proscribed in 1992.

Ulster Defence Regiment (UDR) A regiment of the British Army made up of full-time and part-time members recruited exclusively in Northern Ireland, it was raised in 1970 after the disbandment of the B Specials. In 1992 the UDR was amalgamated with the Royal Irish Rangers to form the Royal Irish Regiment.

Ulster Volunteer Force (UVF) A loyalist paramilitary group claiming descent from Sir Edward Carson's UVF of 1913, but established in modern times in 1966 by Shankill Road loyalists, when it carried out the first killings of the current Troubles. Banned in June 1966, it was legalised in April 1974 before again being declared illegal in October 1975.

Ulster Workers' Council (UWC) It emerged out of the Loyalist Association of Workers to organise the loyalist strike which brought down the power-sharing executive in May 1974.

United Ulster Unionist Council (UUUC) An umbrella group of unionist parties, including the UUP, DUP and VUP, which were opposed to power-sharing. It existed from April 1974 until an unsuccessful DUP-inspired strike in 1977 when the UUP withdrew.

II. The Main Political Parties Involved in the Politics of Northern Ireland

Alliance party   Founded in 1970, a small, middle-class party attracting support from both communities. Based mainly in the greater Belfast area, it normally received 6% of the vote.

Democratic Unionist party   Founded in 1971 by Rev. Ian Paisley and initially known as the Protestant Unionist party, it has opposed any move seen as weakening the position of Northern Ireland within the Union. The DUP attracts a strong working-class Protestant vote and in November 2003 became the largest Unionist party in Northern Ireland.

Fianna Fáil   Translated as 'Soldiers of Destiny', it is the largest of the Irish Republic's political parties. Perceived as being the most republican of the south's large parties, for much of the Troubles it was led by Charles Haughey. His successors, Albert Reynolds and Bertie Ahern, played key roles in the peace process of the 1990s, Ahern signing the Good Friday Agreement with British PM Tony Blair.

Fine Gael   Literally meaning 'Tribe of the Gael', it is the second largest political party in the Irish Republic. In 1985 its leader and then Taoiseach, Garret FitzGerald, signed the Anglo-Irish Agreement with Margaret Thatcher.

Progressive Unionist party   The political wing of the UVF, it is a small political party based mainly in west, north and east Belfast since the early 1970s and receives limited electoral support outside those areas. Its most prominent representatives are David Ervine and Billy Hutchinson.

Sinn Féin Regarded as the political wing of the IRA, it claims descent from the party established in 1904 by Arthur Griffith. It is an all-Ireland political organisation and unique in that it has representation in Dáil Éireann and the House of Commons as well as in the Northern Ireland assembly, although its MPs do not take their seats at Westminster. It aims to create a united thirty-two-county Irish Republic. In June 2001 it became the largest nationalist party in Northern Ireland and in November 2003 the largest nationalist party in the northern assembly. Its leader is Gerry Adams MP.

Social Democratic and Labour party (SDLP) For most of the Troubles the largest nationalist party in Northern Ireland, it was founded in 1970 with aims to promote a united Ireland by peaceful means and agreement. Led from 1979 to 2001 by John Hume MP MEP. He was succeeded by Mark Durkan.

Ulster Unionist party (UUP) The main Unionist party until November 2003 when it was overtaken by Ian Paisley's DUP, the UUP ran Northern Ireland from 1920 to 1972, securing an overall majority at every election. It aims to maintain the constitutional Union with Britain. From 1974 until the early 1990s it was called the Official Unionist party to distinguish it from the various Unionist splinter groups which emerged in the 1970s. It has been led since 1996 by David Trimble MP.

Vanguard Unionist party (VUP) A political party established in 1973 by William Craig, the former Minister of Home Affairs in the Stormont government.

III. Timeline of Key Events

1962

February IRA border campaign ends.

1963

March Terence O'Neill becomes prime minister of Northern Ireland.

1964

September Divis Street riots.

October British general election brings Labour to government.

1965

January Taoiseach Sean Lemass meets O'Neill at Stormont.

February O'Neill meets Lemass in Dublin.

1966

March UVF formed Gerry Fitt elected MP for West Belfast.

April Easter Rising 50th anniversary celebrations north and south.

May 77-year-old Protestant widow fatally burned in UVF petrol-bomb attack.

June UVF shoot dead 2 Catholic men and wound 2 others.

July Paisley imprisoned for unlawful assembly.

1967

January Northern Ireland Civil Rights Association (NICRA) formed.

1968

August First civil rights march, from Coalisland to
Dungannon.

October 77 injured as RUC attack civil rights march in
Derry.

November O'Neill meets prime minister Harold Wilson at
Downing Street. Later announces a reform package.

December O'Neill's 'crossroads speech'.

1969

January PD march from Belfast to Derry ambushed at
Burntollet bridge.

Brian Faulkner resigns from O'Neill's Cabinet.

February O'Neill calls a snap election.

March UVF bombing campaign begins.

April Bernadette Devlin wins Mid-Ulster by-election.
O'Neill resigns.

May James Chichester-Clark defeats Faulkner to become the
North's prime minister.

August Serious rioting in Derry after Apprentice Boys'
march; the RUC uses CS tear gas.

14 August British Army deployed in Derry. Major
disturbances in west and north Belfast.

15 August British Army deployed in west and north Belfast.

September Army erects 'peacelines' in Belfast.

October B Specials abolished. Sir Arthur Young appointed to
modernise RUC.

December The IRA split. Provisional IRA Army Council
established.

1970

January Provisional Sinn Féin founded.

April Ian Paisley elected Stormont MP in a by-election for
O'Neill's old seat.

May Taoiseach Jack Lynch sacks Charles Haughey and Neil
Blaney.

Haughey and Blaney arrested.

June Conservatives win British general election.

July Falls Road curfew.

August SDLP formed, with Gerry Fitt MP as leader.

October Haughey and co-defendants acquitted in Arms Trial.

1971

February First British soldier killed in the North.

March Chichester-Clark resigns. Faulkner becomes PM.

July SDLP withdraws from Stormont.

August Internment. Huge upsurge in violence.

October Dungiven parliament organised by the SDLP.
Rev. Ian Paisley establishes the Democratic Unionist party.

1972

January Bloody Sunday when paratroopers shot dead 13
unarmed civilians in Derry; another died later.

March Stormont abolished; direct rule introduced.

William Whitelaw becomes first secretary of state for
Northern Ireland.

July IRA meet Whitelaw for talks in London. 22 IRA bombs
kill 11 in Belfast's Bloody Friday.
British Army take over so-called No-Go Areas in Derry.

December Bombs explode in Dublin as the Dáil debates
anti-terrorist measures; 2 killed.

1973

January Ireland and Britain join the EEC.

February First loyalists interned.

March Whitelaw publishes his White Paper on future government of the North, mentioning the 'Irish dimension'. June Assembly elections.

December Sunningdale conference sets the scene for power-sharing in the North.

1974

January Power-sharing executive takes office. Faulkner defeated 457-374 by Ulster Unionist Council on the Council of Ireland.

Faulkner resigns as UUP leader and is replaced by Harry West.

February British general election. Labour returned. Anti-Sunningdale Unionists win 11 of 12 seats in Northern Ireland.

March Merlyn Rees becomes secretary of state.

May Ulster Workers' Council strike.

Bombs in Dublin and Monaghan kill over 30 people.

October In British general election anti-Sunningdale Unionists win 10 of 12 seats.

1975

February IRA ceasefire. Incident centres set up.

May Convention elections. Unionists opposed to power-sharing win overall majority.

December Internment ended.

1976

March End of Special Category Status for prisoners.

August The Peace People march.

September Roy Mason becomes secretary of state.
First IRA prisoner after end of Special Category Status refuses to wear prison clothes.
November Peace People leaders win Nobel Peace Prize.
December Fair Employment Act passed.

1977

May Paisley leads another 'workers'' strike. Called off after 10 days.
June Jack Lynch elected Taoiseach.

1978

February IRA firebombing of La Mon hotel.
March The 'dirty protest' begins in jails.

1979

March Conservative Northern Ireland spokesman Airey Neave killed.
May Margaret Thatcher wins British general election.
Humphrey Atkins becomes secretary of state.
August Lord Mountbatten and others killed off Sligo coast on same day as 18 soldiers and a civilian at Warrenpoint.
September Pope John Paul II visits Ireland.
October Atkins announces a political initiative.
November Gerry Fitt resigns as SDLP leader; succeeded by John Hume.
December Charles Haughey elected leader of Fianna Fáil and Taoiseach.

1980

January Atkins round-table conference opens. UUP boycotts it.

March Atkins conference ends.

May First Haughey–Thatcher summit.

October 7 IRA prisoners begin hunger strike for political status.

December Hunger strike called off.

Second Haughey–Thatcher summit agrees joint studies on security and economics.

1981

January Bernadette McAliskey (*née* Devlin) seriously wounded in assassination attempt.

March Second H-block hunger strike starts, led by IRA prison commander Bobby Sands.

April Sands wins Fermanagh–South Tyrone by-election.

May Sands dies after 66 days on hunger strike.

June 2 hunger-strikers elected to the Dáil.

August Sinn Féin candidate Owen Carron wins Fermanagh–South Tyrone by-election.

September Jim Prior becomes secretary of state.

October Hunger strike called off.

November Dublin and London set up Anglo-Irish Intergovernmental Council.

1982

February Irish general election returns Charles Haughey as Taoiseach.

October Assembly elections. Sinn Féin wins 10% of the vote. Nationalists boycott the assembly.

November General election in the Republic; Garret FitzGerald Taoiseach.

1983

May New Ireland Forum meets.

June British general election. Gerry Adams wins West Belfast from Gerry Fitt.

John Hume elected MP in Derry.

September Adams elected president of Sinn Féin.

1984

March Adams shot and wounded by UDA.

May *Forum Report* published.

September Douglas Hurd becomes secretary of state.

October IRA bomb at Conservative party conference at Brighton: 5 dead.

November Thatcher rejects the *Forum Report*'s options.

1985

May Sinn Féin wins 59 council seats in the North.

September Tom King becomes secretary of state.

November Anglo-Irish Agreement signed. Widespread unionist protests.

December All Unionist MPs resign to force by-elections.

1986

January By-elections result in loss of 1 seat to SDLP.

March Unionist 'day of action'. Unionist riots.

August DUP deputy leader Peter Robinson MP arrested after incursion into Clontibret, County Monaghan, by convoy of loyalists.

November Sinn Féin *árd fheis* permits successful Sinn Féin candidates to take Dáil seats. Republican Sinn Féin formed.

1987

March Charles Haughey's Fianna Fáil returned to power.

April Northern Ireland's second most senior judge and his wife killed by an IRA car bomb.

May Sinn Féin publish *A Scenario for Peace*.

8 IRA members shot dead by SAS at Loughgall.

June Thatcher wins her third general election.

SDLP win their third seat, South Down.

November French coastguards intercept the *Eksund* carrying tonnes of weaponry from Libya for the IRA.

Enniskillen Poppy Day bomb kills 11.

1988

January Hume and Adams meet.

March 3 IRA volunteers shot dead in Gibraltar by SAS.

Funerals of those killed in Gibraltar attacked by Michael Stone, killing 3 people and injuring dozens.

SDLP/Sinn Féin talks continue.

August Ballygawley bus bomb: 8 soldiers killed.

September End of SDLP/Sinn Féin talks.

October British announce broadcasting ban on paramilitary organisations and their supporters.

1989

February New IRA campaign in Britain begins.

July Fianna Fáil/Progressive Democrat coalition in the Republic.

Peter Brooke becomes secretary of state.

November Brooke says IRA cannot be defeated militarily and talks with Sinn Féin 'inevitable'.

Sinn Féin launch a revised *A Scenario for Peace*.

Sinn Féin asks for talks with British.

1990

January Brooke begins political talks process.

November Brooke declares Britain has 'no selfish, strategic or economic interest' in Northern Ireland.

Margaret Thatcher resigns.

John Major becomes Conservative party leader and prime minister.

1991

March Brooke issues his 'three-strand' approach to talks and announces suspension of Anglo-Irish conference meetings so that Unionists will attend talks.

April Brooke talks begin without Sinn Féin.

July Brooke talks end without agreement.

1992

January Charles Haughey resigns as Taoiseach, and Albert Reynolds replaces him.

February Sinn Féin publishes *Towards a Lasting Peace in Ireland*.

March 1,000lb bomb in Lurgan. Bombs at railway stations in London.

April US presidential candidate Bill Clinton promises to give Gerry Adams a visa if elected president.

IRA bomb destroys the Baltic Exchange in London and causes almost stg£1 billion damage.

John Major wins British general election.

Gerry Adams loses his West Belfast seat to SDLP.

Sir Patrick Mayhew becomes secretary of state, and restarts

political talks.

August UDA banned.

September 2,000lb IRA bomb destroys Forensic Science laboratories in Belfast and damages 1,000 homes.

October IRA bombs in London.

November Mayhew's talks end fruitlessly.

Fianna Fáil/Labour coalition win general election in Republic.

1993

February UDA attacks SDLP councillors' homes.

April Secret Hume–Adams talks revealed. Hume says the British should 'underline that the Irish people have the right to self-determination.' Hume comes under media attack for talks with Adams.

IRA bomb at Bishopsgate causes millions of pounds worth of damage in London's financial centre, the City.

May 1,000lb IRA bomb in Belfast city centre.

IRA bombs explode in Portadown, Magherafelt and Belfast.

July 1,500lb IRA bomb in Newtownards, County Down.

September Hume and Adams reach agreement and Hume presents it to Irish government.

UDA steps up attacks on SDLP.

October IRA bomb aimed at UDA leaders explodes prematurely killing 9 Protestants and the IRA bomber.

November Secret contacts between IRA and British officials revealed.

December Downing Street Declaration signed by Reynolds and Major in London.

1994

January Sinn Féin seeks 'clarification' of the Declaration.

Reynolds lifts Section 31 ban on Sinn Féin.

President Clinton grants US visa to Adams.

August IRA calls 'complete cessation' of military operations.

September Reynolds, Hume and Adams shake hands outside Government Buildings, Dublin.

Soldiers in the North begin patrolling without helmets.

John Major lifts broadcasting ban on Sinn Féin.

October Loyalists declare ceasefire.

November Reynolds resigns as Taoiseach.

Bertie Ahern elected leader of Fianna Fáil.

December First official meeting between British officials and Sinn Féin.

Decommissioning of weapons becomes major obstacle.

John Bruton of Fine Gael elected Taoiseach, leading coalition with Labour and Democratic Left.

1995

February *Frameworks for the Future* released.

March UUP rejects *Frameworks* document.

Jim Molyneaux re-elected UUP leader, but 15% of votes go to 'stalking-horse' candidate.

July Violent confrontation at Garvaghy Road, Portadown, as Orange Order march is forced through.

August Molyneaux resigns as UUP leader.

September David Trimble MP elected UUP leader.

November President Clinton visits Northern Ireland; shakes hands with Adams.

1996

January Mitchell Commission recommends decommissioning in parallel with talks.

Major announces elections in Northern Ireland.

February IRA ceasefire ends with huge bomb at Canary Wharf, killing 2 men and causing vast damage.

Major and Bruton announce talks on 10 June, excluding Sinn Féin if no IRA ceasefire.

June Talks begin at Stormont, chaired by Senator Mitchell, without Sinn Féin.

July Confrontation at Garvaghy Road.

1997

May Tony Blair wins British general election with record majority.

Adams elected to West Belfast and Martin McGuinness to Mid-Ulster.

Mo Mowlam becomes secretary of state.

June Fianna Fáil/Progressive Democrat coalition wins general election in Republic with Bertie Ahern as Taoiseach.

July IRA ceasefire.

August Independent Commission on Decommissioning led by General John de Chastelain set up.

Mowlam announces Sinn Féin may join talks.

September UUP join talks.

October IRA splits. Minority set up Real IRA.

December Talks adjourn for Christmas break. Jeffrey Donaldson MP and 4 other UUP MPs express concern at direction of talks.

1998

January *Heads of Agreement* paper from two governments.
IRA rejects paper.

April Good Friday Agreement. Jeffrey Donaldson MP
withdraws before signing.

May Agreement endorsed by referenda in north and south:
94% for in south and 71% for in the North, though 50% of
Protestants voted against.

August Real IRA bomb kills 29 people in Omagh.

1999

January Assembly remains stalemated over decommissioning.

September Patten report on policing published.

October Peter Mandelson becomes secretary of state.

November Executive formed from assembly, 10 ministers
appointed.

December North–South ministerial council meets.

2000

February Devolution suspended after threat from Trimble to
resign because of no decommissioning.

May Devolution restored on basis of IRA statement about
weapons and monitoring of arms dumps.

June IRA arms dumps inspected.

2001

June Tony Blair returned to office with large majority in
British general election.
Sinn Féin win 4 seats to SDLP's 3. DUP win 5 seats.

July David Trimble resigns as First Minister.

August Devolution suspended for 1 day to enable 6 weeks of talks.

3 suspected IRA men arrested in Colombia.

September Devolution suspended for 1 day to allow 6 weeks of talks.

October Unionist ministers resign from executive.

IRA begin decommissioning.

November PSNI comes into being.

Executive elected again.

2002

October Executive and assembly collapse after allegations of IRA spyring at Stormont. Tony Blair demands 'acts of completion'.

2003

April Joint Declaration on implementation of Agreement by Irish and British governments.

Adams speech on IRA future fails to satisfy Dublin and London.

Assembly elections due in May are postponed.

October Expected deal between Unionists and Sinn Féin fails to materialise after Unionists reject IRA decommissioning for lack of 'transparency'.

November Assembly elections. Significant gains for Sinn Féin and DUP.

2004

March First talks since assembly elections produce DUP-Sinn Féin deadlock.

September Intensive talks at Leeds Castle stall on DUP terms for IRA decommissioning.

December 'Comprehensive deal' collapses on DUP demands for photos of IRA decommissioning.

£26.5 million Northern Bank robbery blamed on IRA.

2005

March British government says no talks possible until the IRA 'resolves its position'.

May British general election. Gains for DUP and Sinn Féin.

July IRA announces the end of its campaign.

September Decommissioning body announces all IRA weapons decommissioned.

2006

April British and Irish governments present blueprint for restoring devolution.

May Stormont assembly reconvened.

October Intensive talks lead to Irish and British government sponsored St Andrews Agreement.

November Transitional assembly convened.

2007

January Sinn Féin *Ard Fheis* votes to support police.

March Assembly elections. Gains for DUP and Sinn Féin. Paisley and Adams agree on date for devolution.

May Stormont assembly meets. Northern Ireland executive established in presence of Taoiseach and British prime minister.